THE
YOGI BERRA
STORY

B
B45r

By GENE ROSWELL

+

JULIAN MESSNER, INC.

New York

Published by Julian Messner, Inc.
8 West 40 Street, New York 18

Published simultaneously in Canada
by The Copp Clark Publishing Co. Limited

Photographs used with the permission of Wide World Photos

Printed in the United States of America

Library of Congress Catalog Card No. 58—10931

For Rae, Alice and Clint
who made this book necessary

In Appreciation:

Bob Fishel, Bob Dochterman and Don Wiederecht
of the New York Yankees
and Jack Zanger of *Sport Magazine*

· 1 ·

"Hey, ugly, get back in yer tree!"

The derisive cry, echoing from the right field stands at Yankee Stadium, drifted across the outfield grass to a pudgy, forlorn figure in the white flannels of the home team.

From the stands he looked like the caricature of a ball-player, not a major leaguer covering right field for the indomitable New York Yankees in the seventh and deciding game of the 1947 World Series with the Brooklyn Dodgers.

He was shaped wide and low, and his thick arms seemed too long for his squat, deep-chested body.

A ripple of laughter ran through the crowd, spread slowly from section to section and gradually swelled into a roar engulfing the vast ball park and its throng of seventy-one thousand fans.

The stumpy man in right field seemed deaf to the sound. He pounded his fist into his glove and peered grimly toward the plate, where a figure in Brooklyn uniform ambled into the batting box.

It'll soon be over, he thought, the game and the mocking laughs. The shame, too. Only three hits in six games . . . errors, bad throws . . . moved from catcher to outfielder . . . jeers, insults. . . . It had been rough for a young rookie thrust into his first World Series.

From his right he heard a low, firm voice calling, "Yogi . . . Yogi Berra." He turned. Joe DiMaggio, in center, waved him over closer to the stands.

Another boner, Yogi thought. He hadn't noticed Manager Bucky Harris signaling from the dugout to shift with the left-handed batter coming up. Obediently, he changed position, face impassive, almost blank, but cringing inwardly.

Then the inning was over and Yogi trotted back to the dugout. No one had hit to the outfield, much to his relief. He could catch the ball all right, but what to do with it after that was a problem.

The Yankees were up and got a man on base. Berra, up next, walked over to the bat rack. "Hold it, Yogi," said Bucky Harris. "Let's give Clark a crack at these guys."

Yogi said nothing, but the bewilderment and pain of a twenty-two-year-old who felt he had failed was vivid in the downcast eyes and the glum expression. He sat out the rest of the game on the bench, watching mechanically, the joy that should have been his, with the Yankees winning marred by inner gnawings.

The game ended, with the Yankees on top 5–2 and World Champions again, but Yogi couldn't put his heart into the yelling and rejoicing of his teammates. The clubhouse, even for the usually sedate Yankees, was pandemonium this time. It had taken seven games to defeat the Dodgers and the Bombers released their tensions with shouting, back pounding and wild high jinks.

To the disconsolate Berra, the long, wide room with the players' lockers lining the walls was suddenly an alien place. All around him was the excitement of victory, but he didn't feel a part of it. He was the anchor, the kid who had almost thrown it away. All he could think of was to escape, to get away quickly and without notice.

"Brighten up, Yogi," someone shouted across the room, hurling a sopping wet towel that caught him in the back of the neck and left a damp stain on his shirt. "Think of all that dough in your pocket."

Yogi grinned weakly, concentrating on tying his laces. No use feeling sorry for myself, he thought. I just don't have it, that's all. Next year I'll probably be back in the minors . . . the end of my dream.

Like every other kid from The Hill, the Italian section of South St. Louis, Missouri, Lawrence Peter Berra had yearned for a big league career. Every vacant lot, every available plot of grass nurtured budding athletes.

But he and his best pal Joe Garagiola, from across the way on Elizabeth Street, had made it. Joe, tall, handsome and articulate, was last year's World Series hero for the St. Louis Cardinals. But he, Yogi the clown, the butt of the jokes, was the goat of the 1947 classic.

How did it happen? Why? It had been a good season for a rookie. He played in eighty-three games, hit .280, clouted eleven home runs—two of them grand slammers— and drove in fifty-three runs. He had worked himself up from fifth in the Yankee batting order to third.

They said he was a great clutch hitter, an unorthodox swinger against whom no type of pitch was safe. Before the series, Dodger scouts frankly had been worried about Berra—his power, his versatility with the bat and his eye at the plate.

What a laugh, Yogi thought. The only solid clout he got was that pinch-hit homer in the third game, the first time a rookie ever accomplished the feat in a World Series. Otherwise he had been Brooklyn's pigeon at the plate.

The real shame, Yogi knew, wasn't his failure at bat. It was his terrible work as a catcher. He never would forget Jackie Robinson dancing off first base, skittering back and forth, then dashing for second.

It happened in the first inning of the first World Series game in the Stadium, in full sight of more than seventy-three thousand fans. Robbie, an old enemy from the International League, where Jackie played for Montreal when Berra was with Newark, drew a walk in his series debut.

Frank Shea, Berra's roommate, a careful, hard-working right-hander, was pitching for the Yankees. Yogi hadn't been too worried about Robbie. "He never stole on me in the International," the squat catcher had assured Yankee teammates earlier.

But there was Jackie, prancing up and down the base path, annoying Shea. Frank threw to first a few times, but couldn't keep baseball's first Negro player close to the bag. Then it came. Jackie was off like a flash with the pitch, a wide delivery with plenty of room for Yogi to throw.

Hurriedly, he grabbed the ball, ran out two paces and threw. It hit the dirt on the wrong side of second and Jackie was standing on the bag, a big grin on his face as he brushed the dust from his uniform.

The Yanks got Robbie between second and third on Pete Reiser's infield tap, but he scurried back and forth to delay the out long enough for Reiser to reach second. Pete scored before the inning ended, the first run of the series, and Yogi knew it had been his fault.

Jackie drew a pass in the third inning and again his daring tactics bothered Shea. Four times the big hurler snapped the ball over to George McQuinn on first, but the flashy Dodger always came up smiling—and safe.

Berra knew why Shea was working so hard to keep Jackie close to first. Frank had no confidence in Yogi's scatter arm.

Shea stretched for his pitch to Reiser. He glanced over his shoulder at Robbie, edging far off the base, made a move to throw, then checked it.

A balk! The first in Shea's major league career. Jackie trotted cockily to second and Yogi could see Frank's ears redden. Although Reiser flied out to end the inning, Shea strode off the mound grim and angry. Yogi didn't say a word, just dropped onto the bench.

Ralph Branca, the Brooklyn right-hander, was working beautifully. He had struck out Johnny Lindell and Shea in the third, George Stirnweiss and Berra in the fourth. But the Yankees exploded in the fifth with five runs, although Yogi played no part in the rally.

PeeWee Reese stole second on Yogi in the seventh and scored when reliever Joe Page's pitch slipped past the Yankee catcher. In a panic he chased the ball back to the stands, picked it up and threw to Page, covering the plate. The frantic throw was wide and PeeWee scored standing up. The official scorer ruled it a wild pitch, but Yogi felt he should have caught it.

It was like the end of the world to him. "Forget it," DiMag had whispered in the dugout. And when the Yankees won, 5–3, it didn't seem to make any difference.

Manager Harris ambled over as Berra was dressing, noted the catcher's glum face and downcast eyes, but he said nothing. Big leaguers don't need pep talks, he said to himself, but maybe this kid could use one. No, better not, he mused. Might make the kid more nervous. Maybe just drop him down in the batting order tomorrow. Hitting third in a rookie's first series is too much responsibility. Let him bat eighth for the second game and that may take some of the pressure off.

It was a bit of a comedown for the young catcher, but in a way a relief, too. The Yankees were in a clobbering mood for game number two. They pounded four Brooklyn hurlers for fifteen hits and a 10–3 victory. Everybody hit—everybody but Yogi. He swung with wild futility and was just as bad behind the plate with the mask and pads on. Reese stole on him once, and on another occasion Yogi fired a ball past first base to advance the runner. The worst came when he joined with three infielders to gawk at an easy pop-up which fell in front of the plate. Luckily, it bounced foul, but Yogi's feelings weren't salved. He should have taken command and gobbled it up.

Berra's name wasn't in the line-up for the third game at Ebbets Field in Brooklyn. Bucky didn't say anything to him, just posted the list with Sherman Lollar as catcher. Yogi couldn't blame the manager. How many mistakes could a team fighting for the world championship afford from a raw catcher?

Yogi watched the seesaw game from the dugout, not silently but not vociferously either. He didn't shout and jockey like the other bench warmers, just muttered his verbal contribution, fiercely and vehemently. Branca was pitching in the seventh with no one on base and the Brooks ahead 9–7, when Bucky signaled to Yogi.

"Grab your bat," he said. Berra sat stunned for a moment, almost frightened. He felt someone nudge him and hiss, "Get going, kid. Show 'em, boy, show 'em." In a daze he shuffled to the bat rack, picked a club and walked to the plate. He didn't hear the crowd or the taunts from the Brooklyn bench. He just kept staring at Branca.

The lean rightie, a former college athlete at N.Y.U., threw a fast one in, low and away, for a ball. The next was a curve, breaking across the plate for a strike, and Yogi could have kicked himself for letting it go. Branca was fast, but a little wild. Yogi dug in, waiting. The pitcher's arms flashed up, then down, and the ball came in like a streak of white. It was outside and high, but Yogi swung. Crack! The ball arched out toward right field, higher and higher, then disappeared into the crowd. A home run! Jubilantly, Yogi trotted around the bases.

They told him later that it was the first pinch home run ever walloped in a World Series, but he didn't care. The important thing was that he still could hit. He had showed 'em that. The Bombers lost the game, 9–8, and Berra tried to feel bad about it, but he couldn't.

That had been his last proud moment of the series. He caught the fourth game, the one in which the Brooks beat the Yanks, 3–2, after Cookie Lavagetto's blow to right with two out in the ninth inning spoiled Floyd Beven's no-hitter.

Al Gionfriddo, running for Carl Furillo, had stolen second by an eyelash. Then, with the count 3–1 on the lame Reiser, Bucky Harris ordered an intentional walk. Manager Burt Shotton of the Dodgers immediately countered by sending in Ed Miksis to run for Reiser and let Lavagetto hit for Ed Stanky.

Yogi sensed disaster as the ball plummeted off the Dodger third baseman's bat and headed on a line for right field. He watched Tommy Henrich turn and race for the wall, just as earlier in the game he had made a great leaping catch of Gene Hermanski's drive.

But this time the ball soared over Tommy's head, struck the sloping wall and caromed away from his clutching hands. Precious moments were lost as he raced after the ball, finally retrieved it and fired it in. The relay was from McQuinn to the plate—too late.

Gionfriddo and Miksis scored and the game was gone, the series tied at two all, making even the haughty Yankees uneasy. The Dodgers weren't rolling over and playing dead. Yogi realized why he didn't play in the fifth game. It would have been a gamble and he couldn't blame Bucky. The Bombers won, 2–1, as DiMag homered and Henrich doubled to get Shea his win.

The series returned to the Stadium for the sixth game, playing to an enormous throng of seventy-four thousand. It was Branca again versus Allie Reynolds, but this did not turn into a pitching duel. Both teams were clouting. Berra sat on the bench, secretly relieved at escaping the spotlight and yet ashamed of feeling that way.

Then, in the fourth inning, Lindell's bruised ribs began to pain and Harris called Yogi over. "You've got right field," he ordered. Berra's heart jumped. Since he had played the outfield most of the season, at least he couldn't make too many mistakes. Anyway, it would give him a chance to bat.

Yogi got two hits, batting in a run, and was on first when little Gionfriddo made his heroic catch of DiMag's four hundred and fifteen-foot smash to left with two on in the sixth inning. The Bombers lost, 8–6, and the series evened up again at three all. But they came back in championship form to take the seventh and deciding game—1947 World Champions.

And now the series was finished, the season was finished and perhaps Yogi Berra was finished. He sighed sadly, the only man in the Yankee clubhouse with a long face.

A wiry little man with dark, crinkly hair and button-bright eyes strolled over. It was the great Yankee shortstop, Phil Rizzuto, the Scooter.

"When are you going back?" he asked, putting a hand on Berra's shoulder. "Home, I mean."

"I dunno," Yogi mumbled, eyes on the floor. "Tomorrow, I guess. Nothin' to do here any more. Think I oughta pack all my stuff and—?" He looked up with such a doleful expression that Rizzuto couldn't restrain a laugh.

"C'mon feller," he said, tapping Berra's shoulder with his fist. "We're not losing a pisan like you. Your bat's too mean. Plenty of guys who can catch in this country, but not so many who can hit."

He smiled, began to walk away, then paused. "Kid," he said over his shoulder, "you're gonna be a Yankee a long time. See ya."

Did Rizzuto mean it, or was this another gag? The Scooter never pulled that kind of trick, but the naïve Yogi was the butt of a lot of clubhouse jokes. He was so good natured that they just rolled off his back, but this—this was serious.

He had to know. Maybe he was through. There was only one way to find out. Ask the manager. Bucky Harris was in his office, only half dressed, surrounded by friends and well-wishers. Yogi couldn't find the nerve to ask Bucky in front of these people.

He didn't have to. Bucky spotted him first. "Yogi!" he shouted. "Come in, slugger." He got up and put his arm around the rookie. "Folks," he announced, "meet our number one catcher for next season."

The group fell silent for a moment. Yogi's jaw dropped, his mouth open like a fish out of water. Was this a cruel joke? Retaliation against an inept catcher who had almost cost Harris the series? All his thoughts registered swiftly and poignantly on Berra's impressionable face.

Bucky watched with amusement, then concern. "Yes, Yogi," he said. "It means a lot of hard work, but we're going to make you a catcher. Now get along out there and have some fun." He pushed the bewildered Berra through the doorway into the clubhouse.

"You serious, Bucky?" a veteran baseball man asked. "That clown? Do you think he can do it?"

"He'd better. We're counting on him. I know he can

hit. Whether he can catch . . ." Bucky shrugged. He watched Yogi, spirits buoyed, join the celebrants. Berra's plain features, lumpy nose and small, round face were lit in a boyish grin.

"He's not ugly," the manager said. "He could be the most beautiful hitter in baseball."

THE YOUR BERRA STORY

· 2 ·

Pietro Berra sighed as he sank wearily into the wooden armchair with the pillowed seat and slipped off his heavy shoes. It had been another hard day in the brickyard, where the heat of a St. Louis summer seemed to search out a man and broil the strength from him.

He could hear his wife Pauline clattering around in the kitchen and the chatter of the boys getting ready for supper. The plates rattled as his daughter Josie set the table. It was a good life and a good country, he thought, the lines softening his rugged features.

It had been the right thing, leaving bare, starving Italy with his friend Giovanni Garagiola those many years ago for a new life in golden America. Now they worked together in the brickyard and lived across the way from each other in identical yellow brick houses on Elizabeth Street on The Hill.

The Hill, the Little Italy of South St. Louis, seemed almost like the old country, except that people could work and eat steadily here. A man could raise a family without fear of starvation, sickness and a hopeless future.

Josie, a bright-eyed child, came in carrying a glass of red liquid. "Drink, Papa," she said. Tomato juice! He sighed again. An American custom. "Good vitamins," his wife had said. "Wine you can drink with the meal. But before—tomato juice!" He drank. It was nice and cold, anyway.

Strange customs, he thought, in America. Still, they must be better than those he had left across the sea. Look at the children—his own, Giovanni's and all the others who had come from Italy; strong, healthy, full of life. . . .

But there were Americans customs he didn't like. Pietro's eyes saddened. The young ones were more interested in playing than in working, the boys with their sports games, the girls with their dances and movies. Where would it end?

His own boys were the worst. First Tony, wanting to sign with a baseball team which had promised him money for playing. Some team from Cleveland with a crazy name, the Indians or something. Then there was Mike—and later John—with St. Louis teams shoving money at them.

He had stopped that, thank God. Now Tony worked steady in the bakery, Mike was in the shoe factory and John waited on tables down at Ruggieri's restaurant. Good, honest jobs, something to depend on.

The little one, Laudi—no one called him Lawrence Peter—was like the others. He didn't want school. No time for studying, to be smart and learn, maybe become a rich man. Just play, play, play on the ball fields.

At the table, Papa looked around at his sons, noticing the empty place. "Where's Laudi? Playing ball?" It wasn't really a question. "Sh, Papa," his wife said. "Don't get excited. He's a little late."

Supper was finished long before young Berra came home, dirty and exhausted but beaming. "We're in," he said, nudging Mike. They all knew that he meant his team, the Stags, had won the Y.M.C.A. baseball championship.

"Who pitched?" Tony asked, studying his kid brother. Laudi was fourteen now, short but broad in the shoulders, thick through the arms and legs and weighing about one hundred and forty pounds. Kind of homely, too, with a simple, trusting look about him.

"Joey," answered the youngster. He meant Joey Garagiola, his best pal and son of his father's closest friend. He and Joey, tall and flashy looking with a nimble wit and nimbler tongue, were inseparables.

Joey and he alternated at pitching and catching for the Stags. And down at the Italian-American Athletic Club, Berra went in for another sport. He had donned boxing gloves and climbed into the ring on a lark and wound up beating everyone in his class. Fighting, like baseball, was a simple thing—just wade in and hit. He won nineteen of twenty bouts, ten by knockouts, and flattened the boy who beat him the second time around.

Papa Berra put an end to his son's boxing career when he finally heard of it. "No more fighting," he blazed. "No more! Understand?" Young Laudi understood. "Okay, Pa, okay," he agreed. "I'll play baseball. Okay?"

"Okay, okay," the old man mocked fiercely. "Everything okay, okay. All you think about is play. You go to school, learn something. You don't have to work in brickyard or in factory. Get some brains in your head."

"No, Pa, I got enough brains. No more school . . . please," the youngster pleaded. "I want to work . . . anything . . . I'm wasting my time in school."

It was an old argument in the Berra household. Eight years of grammar school had been a boring struggle for Laudi and now that Joey Garagiola and his pals were ready to go into high school, he made up his mind he'd had enough of school. He wanted a job—and more time to play baseball.

Eventually, the old man yielded. "What's the use of forcing him to go to school if he doesn't want it?" Mama had pointed out with patient logic. So the fourteen-year-old shucked off his school ties and became a workingman.

A rugged-looking lad, Larry—"Don't call me Laudi any more"—had no trouble finding jobs. He had worked on a soft-drink truck, in a shoe factory, in a coalyard, as a busboy, but never lasted long in any of them. Baseball interfered with business as much as it had interfered with school.

And young Berra was playing ball more than ever. Leo Browne, a wealthy oilman who managed the Stockham American Legion Post for the love of the game, had spotted Larry and Joe Garagiola and signed them for his team. Berra lacked his buddy's polish, but he was a natural with the bat.

"The kid can hit," Browne told anyone who would listen. "He's a slugger, a murderer. He don't care where you pitch it, he whams it."

He hadn't been impressed with the Berra kid at first, the one they played jokes on all the time. A nice boy, good natured and solidly built, but kind of runty to be playing with the big fellows. His doubts disappeared, however, the first time he played. Incased in that awkward-looking frame was an athlete, someone with special strength, special speed, special instincts.

Browne played Berra behind the bat or in the outfield. He was no ball of fire with the glove, but put a bat in his hand and the manager could watch him all day. He swung it like a warrior's mace, primarily to smash the ball. No grace, no form, and he went for the craziest pitches—inside, outside, high, low—but he usually connected with an impact that sent the ball rocketing.

Like everyone else exposed to Berra, Browne liked the stocky young man with the pleasant grin and the disposition of an amiable puppy. The kid still puzzled him, though. He looked so simple and played so smart. He was a clown off the field, but he never made a wrong move on it.

To Browne and everyone, Berra was Yogi, a strange nickname for a boy from Little Italy. "How'd he get that moniker?" Browne once asked Garagiola. "It doesn't figure."

Joey laughed. "It does," he said, "if you know Yogi."

Browne, interested, eyed Garagiola and waited.

"It was back when we were playing with the Stags. We're all movie nuts, the whole gang, but Yogi is the worst. Well, there was this picture about India with a yogi character in it and when we come out suddenly Laudi looks just like this guy to us and . . . well, what else could we call him after that?"

The manager nodded. Garagiola was right; it did figure.

Once an umpire in the minor leagues, Leo Browne was devoted to baseball. His teams were carefully selected, always did well and his judgment of players was respected by major league scouts who knew him. This was a particularly strong nine. Besides Berra and Garagiola, he had Russ Steger in center, a brute of a lad who later was a star fullback at the University of Illinois.

There was Freddy Hoffman who went to the New York Giants as a second baseman, and Jack Maguire who also got his chance as an outfielder in the Polo Grounds. The Boston Red Sox took Billy Goodwin as a pitcher. Browne not only knew how to pick players, he also knew how to help them further their careers.

By 1942 when Yogi was 17, Browne was convinced that the best position for him was catcher and he arranged for Berra and Garagiola to get tryouts with the St. Louis Cardinals. Both had worked out on occasion for the St. Louis teams, the Cards and the Browns, but this was a real trial.

Yogi and Joey left Elizabeth Street early that summer

day. The sky was a clear, fierce blue from which the sun blazed relentlessly.

"What you got in there?" Joey asked, nodding at the brown paper bag under Yogi's arm.

"Lunch," he answered. "You?"

Garagiola lifted a small, neatly wrapped square for his friend's inspection. Yogi sniffed deprecatingly. "You're gonna be hungry," he warned. "You'll ask me for some, wait and see."

Joey snorted. "I don't want to die young," he said. "I know what's in there."

"Yeah, what?" They both knew, but it gave Yogi pleasure to hear his friend talk.

"Heroes." Garagiola said it flatly, with a certainty born of experience. "Big fat hero sandwiches, enough to feed an army. Ten, I'll bet. What are you gonna do, sell 'em in the stands?"

"Maybe I will, wise guy . . . if there's any left."

Joey gave his best friend a withering look. "Banana and mustard heroes, I suppose."

Yogi sighed. Joey was a real good pal, but he didn't know anything about food. Bananas sliced into a long loaf of Italian bread and smeared with mustard made a delicious repast. Yogi couldn't understand why the combination seemed so ludicrous to others.

Browne was waiting for them at the ball park. "Branch Rickey is here," he told the boys. Rickey was the big boss of the Cardinals, the Mahatma himself, a frightening name to the kids from The Hill. He sat with a group of men in the shaded stands.

Yogi stared unabashed at the man who held the fate of so many baseball players in his hands. He saw a pair of shrewd eyes glittering in a square, wrinkled face, and a straight, narrow mouth from which protruded the largest cigar he had ever seen.

Joey tugged his sleeve. "Stop staring, you dope. He's supposed to look at us, not us at him." Yogi turned away, but not before he received a startlingly solemn wink from the owlish old face.

"Hey, he winked at me," Yogi hissed, nudging Garagiola. "The old guy give me the wink."

Joey gazed at his squat friend with weary patience. "Everybody winks at you, Yogi," he said.

The sun, almost directly overhead, baked the turf to a crisp, but the two young men were too excited to notice the intense heat. Several other candidates were limbering up, tossing a baseball back and forth and stealing nervous glances into the stands where Rickey sat with his entourage.

A tryout is a routine affair. One or more of the big league club's officials directly concerned with obtaining personnel watches the candidate run, throw and bat. The boy is studied for speed of hand and foot, co-ordination and general demeanor.

Garagiola worked first and Yogi could see his friend was doing well. Joey was graceful and quick behind the bat. He connected with several good shots at the plate, and on his speed trial he ran the bases well. Heads around Rickey nodded encouragingly as the judging group conferred. Joey had made it, Berra was sure.

Then it was his turn. Yogi caught one of the Cards' batting practice pitchers, a burly blond man with huge shoulders. "Don't worry, kid," he said. "I'll put it in there and all you do is hang onto it." That part was all right. Yogi could catch anything thrown at him even if he didn't look too certain or too smooth in the process.

It was his own throwing that worried him. His arm had plenty of power but not enough accuracy. Several throws to second base went zooming over the infielder's head. During the bunt drill Yogi pounced on the ball quickly enough, but again his fierce pegs weren't always on target.

At bat, he poled a few real well, but felt himself pressing too hard. "Ease up, ease up," he heard Joey shout. "Just meet the ball." The pitcher was serving it up too slowly and Yogi was too anxious. Finally, it was over.

Yogi was silent as they dressed in the Cardinals' clubhouse. He looked around at the lockers with the major league players' names on them and wondered if his name ever would be there. That was the life! Playing ball every day, traveling in Pullmans, living in the best hotels.

The boys walked out onto the field again. "Well, Leo," Garagiola asked, "how's it look?"

Browne shrugged. "Ask them," he said, nodding toward Rickey and his group. "He wants to see you both in his office. You go first, Joe."

Yogi flicked the pages of a magazine in the waiting room as his friend conferred with Rickey in his office. When the door opened, Yogi knew. Joey's face was flushed and his grin went from ear to ear.

"They signed me, Yogi, for their Springfield farm club ... with a five hundred dollar-bonus. Brother! That pays off the mortgage. Wait till Pop hears this." Then, grasping Yogi's shoulder, he added, "It's your turn, kid. Good luck."

Yogi felt as he had one time in the principal's office at Wade Grammar School—scared and cold. Although Rickey looked stern, he was nice. "Sit down, young man," he said benevolently. "Let's have a chat."

Berra sank into the leather armchair opposite the man who commanded the St. Louis Cardinals. Lively eyes peered at him from beneath huge quizzical eyebrows. Rickey puffed on a cigar while they sat in deep silence for a while.

"Young man," he said, "I'll be frank with you. I admire your spirit. You show the right attitude. You want to play, and that's half the battle."

He beamed and Yogi's hopes soared.

"But"—and Rickey paused to waggle his cigar at Berra—'there's the other half. You're too small, for one thing, and wild, for another. Come back in another year or so. . . ." He smiled, like a principal again.

Yogi swallowed hard. "Mr. Rickey, I want to play ball . . . I gotta. . . . Can't you find a place for me somewhere . . . anywhere?" His world was collapsing around him. "My friend . . . Joe Garagiola, you know. . . ."

Rickey waved the cigar. He understood. The kid couldn't go back as a failure to the same block with the successful neighbor. He ruffled some papers on his desk. "There's a club. . . ." He mentioned a name that Yogi, groggy with renewed hope, didn't catch. "We can't pay much, but if it makes you feel better, all right."

There was one more thing Yogi had to do. He swallowed again, eyes downcast, then plunged ahead: "What about a bonus?"

Rickey pushed back from his desk in astonishment, his mouth agape. Then he smiled magnanimously. "I admire your courage," he said. "That alone is worth two hundred dollars."

Somehow Yogi found the strength to shake his head. "I'm sorry, Mr. Rickey," he muttered. "I gotta get five hundred dollars . . . like Joey."

Rickey's face grew troubled. He took the cigar carefully from his mouth and put it down in an ash tray on his desk. "Mr. Berra, I'm afraid this negotiation has gone far enough," he said, his mouth tight and his eyes sad. "It wouldn't be fair to the club and our stockholders. Frankly, and I say this for your own good, I don't think you can ever be a major league ballplayer. You're not built for this game.

"Don't waste your time," he added in a kindly tone. "Get a job, stick to it and make something of yourself." He stood up. The interview was ended.

"Sorry," he said, extending his hand. Yogi shook hands limply, numb with surprise and despair. He couldn't believe it. Joey on his way into the big league. He, Yogi Berra, not good enough.

It was the end of the world for him.

"Don't worry, kid," Browne consoled Yogi on the way out. "There are other teams."

Berra moved along like a whipped puppy. Joey, the edge taken off his own triumph, put his arm around Yogi. There was nothing to say.

They walked out of the ball park into the midday heat, still carrying their lunch packages. It was not a time for food.

· 3 ·

Leo Browne looked at the big man sitting in his office. Johnny Schulte, the Yankee coach, had come here because he was a friend.

"You won't be sorry," Browne said. "The kid ain't much to look at, but he can hit. That's what you want, isn't it?"

Schulte nodded. He had gone through this a thousand times. Sometimes it paid off, like striking oil or finding gold. And Leo wasn't the kind to get excited over a false alarm.

"Well," Schulte said, rising, "let's take a peek at this Yogi of yours."

It was the third inning when they arrived at the game. Stockham was ahead, 2–1, and had just put a man on base, with Yogi coming up.

"That's Berra," Leo said.

Schulte studied the gnomelike figure approaching the plate, swinging two bats easily and loosely. The kid didn't look big enough, he thought, but there is something about the way he handles those clubs. . . .

The rival pitcher knew Berra well enough to keep the ball away from him. The first two pitches were wide and low. Yogi was eager and full of beans. He fidgeted and squirmed in the batter's box, waved his bat and kept up a steady stream of chatter with the opposing catcher.

The pitcher's third delivery was high and outside, but not out far enough. Yogi's bat swung in a fast, lopsided arc. The ball shot out to left field, higher and higher—over the fence. A homer!

"See what I mean," said Browne, poking the scout. "No form, but plenty of power."

Schulte grunted. He saw, all right. The kid was a slugger. But what kind of a ball was that to hit?

Leo read his friend's mind. "Don't worry. With Yogi there's no such thing as a safe pitch. He goes for bad pitches . . . except for him they're not bad. He clobbers 'em."

Berra was up two more times, lashing a double to right and a triple over the center fielder's head. Not once did he get a chance at a pitch over the plate.

The two men remained in the stands after the others had left.

"He's not much of a catcher," Schulte said.

Browne agreed. "So what? Where do you see hitters like him? You've got to take a gamble on a boy like this. He can learn everything else."

Schulte didn't need convincing. Berra's bat talked loud enough for him. "Okay," he said. "Get the kid. I'll sign him."

Browne smiled. "You'll never regret it. But there's one thing. . . ."

Ah, a catch. Schulte knew it!

"You've gotta give this kid a five-hundred-buck bonus," Leo said. "Same as his pal Garagiola."

Schulte let out a sigh of relief. That was easy.

Yogi rushed home early. He had to get hold of his brothers before Pop heard about it. They would have to do the selling job.

"Don't worry," Tony told him. Mike and Johnny looked grim and determined. Pop had stymied them, but he wasn't going to keep Laudi out. It would be a terrible mistake to keep the kid from his chance.

It was a long, heated argument after dinner that night.

"But Pa," Tony pleaded, "this is what he's gotta do. This is his life. It's a chance at big money. It's a career, not just play."

Mike joined in. "It's business, just like the brickyard, the shoe factory, the restaurant. People pay to see baseball. Every day, six months a year. Look at the money Musial makes. DiMaggio . . . Rizzuto. . . ."

"Good Italian boys," Johnny chimed in. "Respectable and rich."

Yogi pleaded with tears in his eyes. "Pop," he begged, "say it's okay. Say it. The five hundred is yours. All my money."

Pietro Berra stormed and raged. No, he wouldn't let his boy become a bum, a ballplayer, a racketeer. But he looked at his four sons, so earnest in their argument; good boys, all of them. Was he a father not to trust his own flesh and blood?

Mama delivered the clincher. "Pietro," she said, "let him try. This once. Look at Joey. . . ." She waved a hand in the direction of the Garagiolas.

Giovanni's son was sending home money every month. He was happy. He was well. This was a different land. Different ideas. Maybe—

Finally the older man capitulated. His son Laudi was to become a Yankee. The word sounded strange on his lips. Everyone laughed. Josie wrapped her arms about her father and kissed him.

Yogi wept a little and his brothers pounded his back. It

was a night to remember in the Berra household on Elizabeth Street on The Hill.

Yogi grinned happily as he rode the train to Norfolk, Virginia, in the spring of 1943. His friends and relatives had seen him off in a gala farewell, loaded him with candy, fruit, sandwiches. He was on his way.

The United States had been at war since December 7, 1941. The draft was draining organized baseball of its young men, as it did in all other sports and businesses. Otherwise, a raw rookie of eighteen like Yogi Berra would not be headed so soon for a Yankee farm club in the Class B Piedmont League.

The pay was ninety dollars a month. Not much, Yogi knew. It was less than he could earn at home in St. Louis. And he'd have to pay for his room in Norfolk. Seven bucks a week, they had written him, in a boardinghouse that took in ballplayers. He would be riding buses and grabbing meals in diners.

A tough life, someone said, but Yogi never could believe that. It was a life of baseball, playing every day. Who cared about money . . . a room . . . food? The wonderful feeling bubbled up inside him and ran over, pouring out with a laugh of pure elation.

People on the train stared at him, but Yogi didn't care. He glanced at his luggage overhead and chuckled again. In it was a letter from Branch Rickey, now with the Brooklyn Dodgers, inviting him to their Bear Mountain camp— and a railroad ticket had been enclosed.

Joey Garagiola was playing for Columbus in the American Association, one step away from the big leagues. His pal would make it, Yogi knew, and so would he. Maybe someday they would be together on the same team. . . .

Norfolk wasn't much of a town, but Yogi didn't mind.

He was homesick for a while, but overcame it. Although he was naïve and quiet, people liked him. In the clubhouse, some of the players made fun of him, yet it was all pleasant; he didn't mind jokes or kidding.

He wasn't a wise guy. Baseball was a serious thing with him. Some of the people in it were rough, even brutal in their attitude to others, but it didn't seem to touch or change the kid from The Hill. He had a gentle approach, even to those who made fun of him or played mean tricks.

Yogi was the character who would find soap in his glove, a garter snake in his shoes, his spikes nailed to the floor. It was always a gag. He smiled and took it. At least he was one of them, a member of the team, and if this was the way they wanted to show their liking, it was fine with him.

It wasn't a great season for Yogi. He caught one hundred and eleven games and batted a meager .258, but there were stretches when the enormous power of his bat burst through. It erupted in a two-day stretch for a total of twenty-three runs driven in: thirteen the first day on two homers, two doubles and two singles; and for ten more the next day on a homer, two doubles and a single.

The Yankee brass, checking reports, were impressed by Berra's clouting. He was assigned to their Kansas City Triple-A farm for 1944. But they reckoned without Yogi's patriotic urge.

All of the boys were going into the service. Back home on The Hill, most of the fellows were gone. Joey went into the Army and for Yogi that was it. The next day he was down at the recruiting station and had entered the Navy.

Things moved swiftly for the moon-faced kid with the big shoulders and stumpy legs: boot training at Bainbridge, Maryland, and, of all places, Norfolk at the Little Creek base, not as a ballplayer this time, but as a navy gob, training for a bigger battle.

The war was a quick kaleidoscope for Yogi, a flying pin wheel of people, places, hard work and, finally, fighting. He was sent overseas for duty on a rocket boat and action in the Normandy landing. It was a small craft, a six-man affair on which Yogi grimly fired a machine gun or helped load the rocket guns.

He was a good sailor, a rugged, capable young man who obeyed orders, kept his mouth shut and did his duty. In time, the overseas assignment ended and Berra came back to the States for a thirty-day leave. It was good being home with the folks, to wander around The Hill, the streets, the shops, the movie houses and the lots where he had played ball as a boy.

He was somebody now in his neat blue uniform, with his manly air and his baseball background, even if it was only minor league so far. He caught his father's eye on him occasionally, proud and puzzled. To the elder Berra, base ball still seemed a strange way to make a living. Perhaps the foolishness would pass now that Laudi was growing up.

All good things come to an end, however, and one day Yogi picked up his new orders to find that he was assigned to New London, Connecticut. That's the submarine base he gasped, thunderstruck! He hadn't volunteered for under sea service . . . it must be a mistake. No mistake, they told him. Just report—on time.

The receiving officer at New London grinned wickedly when he heard Yogi's fears. "You've got it soft, sailor," he said. "You're in the Welfare and Recreation section. You're a baseball player, it says here," the officer concluded with a disdainful glance at the dumpy-looking young man with the worried face.

The base had a strong team, Berra heard. Jimmy Glea son, who had played for Cincinnati and the Chicago Cubs managed the club, which included several major leaguers

Walt Masterson of the Red Sox pitched and so did Gene Thompson of the Reds and later the Giants; Joe Glynn, a Yankee property, was catcher.

Gleason was batting grounders to his infielders when Yogi approached gingerly. It was a while before the manager noticed him.

"Yeah?" he questioned, with a quizzical squint at the strange figure standing woefully before him.

"I'm reporting, sir," Berra managed to say. "For the team . . . I'm assigned to it."

Gleason directed a weary glance skyward. What these guys wouldn't do to get out of slop detail! "Look, kid," he said kindly, "this is for ballplayers. See out there?" he added, pointing to the men on the diamond. "They're pros . . . real ballplayers."

"Yeah, sure," Berra eagerly agreed. "That's why I'm here. The Yankees got me . . ."

"The who?" Gleason exploded. This was the limit. He turned away and resumed his fungo chores.

Crestfallen, Berra watched him uncertainly for a moment. He had his orders. He belonged on the team. He went into the dressing room, wangled a uniform and trotted out to the field again.

Gleason ignored him, but Yogi chased flies in the outfield, grabbed a catcher's mitt and warmed up pitchers, occasionally managing to sneak into the batting cage for a few swings at the ball.

During games, he was a permanent bench warmer. Gleason tolerated him for his battle record but couldn't accept the awkward young man as an athlete.

Berra didn't relish his inactive status—he wanted to play. But this was better than whatever petty chores the Navy would have him doing elsewhere. So he sat.

One hot day, in the tenth inning of a ball game that had

almost emptied the bench, Gleason desperately needed a pinch hitter. His eyes roved the bench, frantically seeking a left-handed batter. No one, he fumed silently, no one . . . but wait . . . let's put that clown in. Might as well.

"Berra!"

Yogi jumped as if given an electric shock.

"You're hitting," Gleason growled. "You're a ballplayer . . . you say. A Yankee, huh?"

The prospect of action roused Yogi. He grabbed a bat from the pile and raced to the plate. He didn't know whether Gleason was kidding or not, but this was a chance he couldn't pass up.

The pitcher, a tall, skinny right-hander with a lot of speed, surveyed the pinch hitter who resembled a sack of potatoes in baseball flannels.

"What's the Navy come to?" jibed the catcher as Yogi dug his cleats into the box. "Are you a sailor, sonny?"

For once Berra didn't feel like chatting. He wanted to hit. It felt nice gripping a bat and waiting for a pitch. Just let this guy put one near the plate. . . .

The hurler took his stretch, reared back and smoked one across the plate like a bullet. Strike one!

Gleason groaned.

Yogi dug in harder, waggled his bat and waited.

The next pitch was fast, but low and straight for his ankles. He swung his bat viciously, like a golfer blasting out of a sand trap. There was a sharp crack and the ball shot out, picked up height and disappeared into the trees well beyond the right fielder. It was a home run—and the ball game.

Gleason clapped his hands to his head. "How do you like that?" he yelled to one in particular. "This is the luckiest bum. . . . Oh, brother, now I've seen everything."

Yogi didn't get into the next game or the one after that.

One lucky blow doesn't make a slugger, Gleason lamented. The kid's just a phony, riding it out on the ball team.

Two weeks later the New London nine was in the same spot—a late inning, no one on the bench but Yogi and a hit needed.

"Okay, Yankee boy," Gleason shouted. "Let's see you smack one now."

"Yes, sir." Grinning happily, Yogi took his time selecting a bat and ambled to the plate. Gleason almost blew a gasket watching the act.

The pitcher studied the batter for a moment, took a fast windup and let fly. The delivery was high and so far out that Yogi almost fell over as he slashed at it. The ball seemed to explode, then went whistling past the center fielder before he could move for it.

Another homer and another game won by Yogi.

He accepted the handshakes and joyous back pounding shyly. Gleason, walking back to the lockers, beckoned him over.

"What kind of a pitch did you hit, kid?" he asked.

"High and outside, coach."

"Do you think the Yankees are gonna take a guy who swings at a ball like that?"

Yogi shrugged. "Coach, I see 'em, I hit 'em!"

Gleason sighed. This kid was too much for him. "Okay, okay. From now on, you start." He paused, watching Berra's eyes widen as realization sank in.

It's gonna be tough on our pitchers with him catching, Gleason mused. But it'll be tougher on the other pitchers . . . I hope.

· 4 ·

Larry MacPhail, president of the New York Yankees, was poring through a pile of papers on his huge desk in the club's sumptuous Fifth Avenue office when the intercom buzzed.

"Mr. Ott to see Mr. MacPhail," the receptionist trilled.

Mel Ott, former Giant home run king, came in, a big grin creasing his open features. Mel now managed the Polo Grounds team and the big, redhaired MacPhail knew this was no social visit.

"You're pretty well fixed for catchers, aren't you, Larry?" Ott asked, relaxing in a leather armchair.

MacPhail nodded, rubbing his nose thoughtfully. He had four on the Yankee pay roll.

"We'd like to buy one of 'em," Ott continued. "A kid you probably don't even know you've got."

"Who?"

"His name is Berra, just out of the Navy. Look, Larry, let's save time. We'll give you fifty thousand for him."

A red light flashed in MacPhail's brain. He couldn't recall the name, but if the Giants wanted him fifty thousand dollar's worth, it required more than snap judgment.

"Not that kid, Mel," MacPhail said slowly. "He's real good. Let me think it over."

After Ott had gone, MacPhail was on the phone in a hurry, clamoring for information on Berra. "Get the files on this guy," he roared. "Get Krichell, get Schulte, get anyone."

It didn't take long to get Yogi Berra himself into the Yankee offices for inspection by MacPhail.

"Let's see what my fifty-thousand-dollar baby looks like," he chuckled, rushing out with expectations high to meet the highly touted catcher.

His face fell as he saw the chunky little fellow in a Navy uniform smiling uncertainly at him. MacPhail glanced at his prize with a sinking feeling. The kid's got no neck, was the first thought running through his mind.

Their conversation was mostly a monologue by MacPhail with Yogi saying little more than yes, sir and no, sir. Finally, MacPhail gave up.

When Berra had left, the Yankee president kicked himself mentally for turning down Ott's offer. This, surely, was no ballplayer. "But," he admitted resignedly, "I'm stuck with him. . . ."

Unimpressed as he was with Yogi Berra's physical appearance, the astute MacPhail realized that a man with Ott's baseball knowledge didn't toss fifty-grand offers around for laughs. The best way to find out was to bring Berra up to a club where he could be watched closely.

MacPhail pressed a button summoning his secretary, who came in pad in hand. "Take a note to Paul Krichell," he said. "Move Lawrence Berra up to Newark."

The girl waited for more. "That's all," MacPhail ordered, waving her out. The rest, he knew, would be up to the odd-shaped kid.

The Newark Bears, Yankee farm club in the International League in 1946, was just one step away from the majors. Here was the final test for the skilled, lucky ones aspiring to wear the New York uniform in Yankee Stadium. Here, also, was where the skidding veterans stopped on their way down the ladder again.

The decision to send Berra to Newark was a hasty one. The Bears, when Yogi finally caught up with them in Rochester, had never heard of him. They had expected Walt Dubiel, a pitcher moving up the ladder, but Berra was a surprise.

There was some confusion and embarrassment before Yogi, stranded in the hotel lobby like a displaced person, was accepted as a ballplayer. He had to prove it by burrowing into his luggage for the contract which assigned him to his new team.

"Get him a room," George Selkirk, the Newark manager, finally growled. He was tired and it was late. The Bears were on an important road trip that could decide the pennant, with another ten days to play before they would be home.

At the ball park the next day, Yogi was largely ignored. The trainer had pieced together an outfit from some old uniforms so that Yogi, at least, could sit with the team.

The trainer, an old fellow with cynical eyes, obviously didn't think much of the newcomer's chances to stay on—or even his right to Newark equipment. The shirt was too small, the pants too large. Yogi accepted them mildly, but the cap, a faded, frayed travesty, was too much.

"Get me a better one," he ordered, surprised at his own audacity. "If I'm good enough for this club, I'm good enough for a decent cap."

One look at the rookie's angered expression and the equipment man pulled out a new cap and handed it to Yogi. He'll give it back soon, the trainer thought as he watched the chunky rookie clap the hat defiantly on his head and wander off to a locker.

Berra did nothing during the entire trip but take up space on the bench. A team on the road has precious little practice time and the most Yogi could do was to toss the ball around in the warm-up period.

Selkirk, managing the Bears after a career with the Yankees where he had been the first outfield replacement for the immortal Babe Ruth, had no choice with the newcomer. He just couldn't throw an untested unknown into the line-up.

Yogi was an unhappy man on the trip, lonely and lost. He hung around the batting cage during pregame practice, wistfully eying the regulars taking their licks, hoping someone would take pity and invite him to belt a few.

It never happened. Professional baseball players live on their hits and no one ever gives away a moment in the cage. The players treated him nicely, but he was new, strange to them and to his surroundings. The Bears, battling for first place, were absorbed in problems more important than the social well-being of a raw rookie.

It was better when the team finally returned to Newark. Yogi roomed with Bobby Brown, a good-looking, studious infielder considered a tremendous prospect. Best of all, now Yogi could go to the park mornings and get some action.

Selkirk was leaning against the rail behind the batting cage, talking to Buddy Hassett, his first baseman, when Yogi finally came up for his turn. The manager gazed with mild interest as the squat rookie dug in at the plate and wiggled his bat, waiting for the delivery.

Yogi smashed the first shot close to the light tower in right field, almost out of the park. Hassett stared at the funny little fellow with the big, chopping swing. Selkirk suddenly was all eyes. Yogi hammered the next one into the stands. He hit screaming liners and towering drives, and play ceased all around the stadium as others paused to watch.

Joe Collins, a burly outfielder destined for a slugging role with the Yankees later on, shook his head in amazement. "I'd never have believed it," he told Allie Clark, another outfielder, "if I didn't see it." Allie agreed.

Selkirk was enthralled. A long-ball hitter himself, he could appreciate the dynamite in this awkward-looking youngster's thick shoulders and his ferocious swing. The kid lunged for balls over his head, stretched for wide ones and golfed the low ones in the dirt. But he connected— consistently and with power.

"I don't care how or what he goes for," Selkirk argued later with his coaches. "This guy blasts 'em and that's what counts. Don't fiddle around with his form. Just get him in the line-up and let him be."

Berra was a regular from then on. He became acclimated to Newark, liked it almost as much as St. Louis. He could be happy if people were pleasant, there was food to eat, comic books to read and movies to watch.

Best of all, he was playing regularly. There were some mishaps. An all-out performer, Yogi broke his wrist in a collision at home plate, sprained an ankle, was spiked in the head and hurt his thumb, reducing him to seventy-seven games for the season.

The reports to the parent club on this fantastic fifty-thousand-dollar unknown were like electric jolts. Yogi, who had played ten games in the outfield and the rest behind the plate, belted International League pitching for a .314 batting average, including fifteen homers and fifty-nine runs driven in.

Larry MacPhail, shuffling through the pile of papers on his desk, hadn't forgotten Yogi Berra when he sat down with George Weiss and Bucky Harris, his front-office men, to discuss the rookie crop.

"We're bringing Bobby Brown and Frank Colman up for the last couple of days," Harris told his boss. The Yankees, in third place, trailing the Boston Red Sox by seventeen games, had one more week of the 1946 season left.

It had been a strange and distorted campaign in which Joe McCarthy, a great manager over many years, had left. Bill Dickey, one of the finest hitting and fielding catchers in baseball history, had taken over temporarily. He didn't want the job and at this point it was already understood that Bucky Harris, who once had piloted the Washington Senators, would take over in 1947.

"How about a look at Berra?" MacPhail asked. "Selkirk is raving about him."

"He's awfully green," Weiss pointed out. "He needs all the seasoning he can get."

"Sure," answered the redheaded president, "but it won't hurt to have him here a while. And we can always send him back. I've got a hunch about this feller. . . ."

It was Yogi's first glimpse of the fabled Yankee Stadium, that vast steel and concrete bowl which stands athwart the Harlem River in the lower Bronx. It looked immense, with a lush green lawn running four hundred sixty-one feet out to the center field stands.

Yogi Berra, Bobby Brown and Frank Colman stood in the empty grandstand above the Yankee dugout. It was Sunday morning, hours before the week-end double-header, and the park was empty except for some workers near the concession stands and a few laborers smoothing out the diamond.

"This is it," murmured Colman, a strapping outfielder

who hit a hard ball. "The big time." Brown nodded, his intelligent eyes devouring the place.

Yogi broke the rapt silence. "I'm hungry," he said. "Wonder if these guys'll sell me some franks now." He had seen enough of the field, noted the 296-foot marker on the right field wall and knew it was for him. There was nothing romantic or awe inspiring about a 296-foot fence.

Brown laughed. "I'll buy," he said with an amused wink at Colman. "Yogi is the practical one here. If he doesn't keep his strength up, how is he going to blast 'em over the fences?"

Frank Colman grimaced. "Yeah, strength in hot dogs! Who can eat now?"

Berra shrugged. No sense in being nervous. There was plenty of time for that later on when they were out on the field. Now was the time to eat.

Bobby put his arm around Yogi's shoulders. "Come on," he said. "Let's feed the inner man." They started up the steps to the cavernous rear of the grandstand where the refreshment stands were located.

"What's the big fuss?" Berra demanded fretfully. "Everyone's gotta eat. . . ."

For the first time in his life, Yogi felt like a real ball-player. He was a major leaguer now. Sitting in the Yankee dugout as the Philadelphia Athletics limbered up on the diamond and a crowd of twenty-four thousand bustled in the stands, the kid from The Hill proudly fingered the clean flannel uniform with New York emblazoned across the chest.

From time to time he sneaked glances at the men who until now had been just glamorous names in the sports pages: Joe DiMaggio, solemnly chatting; Tommy Henrich, serious but animated; peppery George Stirnweiss, beetle-browed Charlie (King Kong) Keller—all real and within reach.

Berra noticed a slight commotion in the dugout near the entrance to the underground passage to the clubhouse. Bobby Brown came over, trying to seem calm but obviously excited.

"Know what that is?" he asked, flipping a thumb back toward the other side of the dugout. Yogi shook his head.

"It's today's line-up," Bobby said tensely.

Yogi shrugged. "So what?"

"I'm starting at third base," Brown added.

Yogi stared up at his roomie. That's why the guy is so nervous, he thought. "Good luck, Bobby," he said, hiding the envy he felt.

Brown's grin almost split his face. "And good luck to you, too. You're catching."

"What!" Yogi jumped up so suddenly that his head cracked against the low dugout ceiling. He raced to the other end and stared at the small white card tacked on the wall. There was his name: Berra, c., batting eighth.

Yogi discovered that he was nervous, worse than ever in his life. Worse than being in that rocket boat off the coast of France, with bullets whistling about him and the big guns going off.

He struggled futilely with his shin guards. His fingers seemed to be all thumbs. He couldn't get his chest protector on properly. The sweat trickled down his face, his heart pounded wildly and he was afraid he wouldn't be able to walk out to the plate.

"Hello, kid," a soft southern voice drawled. It was Spud Chandler, husky, open-faced pitcher trying for his nineteenth win today.

"Nothin' to it, honest. You just call 'em. If I don't like

'em, I'll just shake you off until we get the right one. Now
don't fret. I got the book on all these swingers."

It was easier than Yogi thought. Chandler was a pleasure
to handle, always around the plate, always pitching to weaknesses.

The big moment for Yogi was his first time at bat against
major league pitching. Jess Flores, a wily left-hander, was
on the mound for the A's.

Berra waddled to the plate, waving a couple of bats. He
threw one away and stepped into the box. Buddy Rosar, a
former Yankee, was the Philadelphia receiver.

"Hey, look at that runt," shouted someone on the A's
bench.

"Does your mama know yer out?" another yelled.

Flores wound up and pitched a strike low and across the
knees. Yogi stepped out of the box, then back into it. He
looked off to right field, hitched his trousers, hunched his
shoulders, squirmed and wiggled.

"Hey, we got a snake dancer," came the next jibe.

Yogi concentrated on the pitcher. Flores reared back.
The pitch was a low curve. Yogi waited until the last frac-
tion of a second, then snapped his wrists and leaned into
the ball. It was a clean smash that cleared the right field
barrier and went into the stands.

His first time up in the majors and Berra had walloped a
homer—with a man on, to boot.

In a box seat over the dugout, MacPhail turned to Bucky
Harris. "That doggoned Ott," he said, "offering only fifty
grand for this kid!"

Berra got another hit, a single, as the Yanks won, 4–3.
Two days later he caught Vic Raschi, rawboned right-
hander just up from Newark, in a 9–6 win. This time Yogi
went two for four, with a homer and a single.

MacPhail was delirious with joy at his new slugger.

Dickey, who resigned as manager the day before but remained on as a coach, was delirious, too, but in reverse. "His catching," Big Bill moaned.

Yogi finished the 1946 season with the Bronx Bombers, playing in seven games, batting .364 and socking two homers.

MacPhail was in the clubhouse when Berra plodded in after the final game of the season. "You're a Yankee from now on, sailor," he bellowed.

Yogi sighed happily. It would be nice going back to The Hill as a major leaguer. Now he wouldn't be embarrassed by Joey, a real big leaguer with the pennant-winning Cardinals. He couldn't wait to get home.

· 5 ·

Yogi was an instantaneous hit with the players and the newspapermen during spring training in 1947.

The sports writers recognized him as wonderfully human and colorful copy, a character with everything an editor could want to enliven his pages. The kid was droll, a clown with muscles, unbelievably naïve, skirting between pathos and humor and always bobbing up with the right word or the right hit.

The Yankees junketed through South America, Cuba and Puerto Rico that spring, with Yogi gawking at places and people he had never dreamed of before. His teammates gawked at him, some amused and tolerant, a few unintentionally cruel in their jokes, but all of them liking this good-natured little fellow who accepted the gibes and antics with grace.

The reporters often were brutal in their coverage and hunt for anecdotes. They described Berra as knock-kneed, stumpy, a gorilla in flannels. They picked up innocuous things he said and exaggerated them into whoppers. They pounced on his every word and every action.

Yogi was bewildered at the reams of space that he, a rookie, commanded in the papers. Joe Garagiola, training with the Cardinals in St. Petersburg, consoled his pal. It had been a great year for Joey, who came out of the 1946 World Series triumph over Boston as something of a young hero.

"Yogi, you just keep hitting," he advised. "That's all you have to do. Let 'em build you up as a character or anything else. It'll mean more money someday."

So Berra took it. There was nothing else he could do. To the rest of the world, his open grin and quick amiability in the face of ridicule, laughter and taunts seemed to signify a callousness to verbal barbs.

But underneath it did hurt. Yogi was sensitive and had sharp ears, but he had come up in a hard school and knew the protective armor of silence. His own bubbling good nature and complete lack of guile was sufficient salve.

"Aw," he shrugged when some of his teammates felt the abuse had gone too far, "they really like me. I'm playing baseball, ain't I?—and that's enough."

It was impossible to dislike this friendly man with his air of perpetual boyish wonderment and his wholehearted enjoyment of baseball. The Yankees began to feel for him a deep affection bordering on admiration.

They laughed at the stories which revolved about Yogi, but they couldn't laugh at him. Thanks to the sports writers, by midspring he had become a stock figure of the baseball character found in Ring Lardner fiction.

His addiction for comic books and the paradoxical fate which roomed him with Bobby Brown, an aspiring doctor boning his way through medical school between seasons, was considered hilarious.

One night in Newark after a grueling double-header, Yogi and Bobby rested quietly in their room reading.

Slowly, Yogi's head drooped and his eyes closed. Soon he was sound asleep. Bobby, immersed in the study of anatomy, was oblivious to Berra's gentle snores. Finally, with a yawn, he banged his book shut. Yogi awoke with a start, noted Bobby had finished reading and dreamily asked: "How'd it come out?"

There was a story that went the rounds about his complaining to Frank Scott, the Yankee road secretary, about the absence of a bed in his hotel room. He was told to pull down the Murphy folding bed from the wall. Ten minutes later Scott heard from Yogi again, this time insisting he wouldn't take a chance sleeping in one of those contraptions. "It might snap up with me in it," Yogi was supposed to have complained.

Actually, these weren't entirely spurious tales. There usually was a small kernel of truth which had either been distorted accidentally or deliberately exaggerated to comic proportions. Yogi's talk and actions did seem to lend themselves to humorous interpretation.

In spring training, one of the liveliest topics was Berra's penchant for swinging at anything thrown his way. The pitch didn't have to be over the plate or, for that matter, even close. Bucky Harris worked assiduously on this fault.

"I know, I know," Yogi agreed when the manager patiently pointed out the advantages of waiting it out for a base on balls, how it would help his batting average, how the pitcher couldn't keep walking him but would have to serve up good ones eventually.

"But I can't help it," Yogi explained. "When I see 'em, I go for 'em. They don't look bad to me."

It inspired the anecdote that Bucky begged him to think at the plate. "Think, Yogi. Think before you swing," Bucky is supposed to have pleaded. After swinging late and striking out, Berra strode back in disgust, muttering: "How's he expect me to think and hit the hall at the same time?"

It didn't happen, but it sounded so much like something Yogi would do that the tale was easy to believe. In fact, it was what people wanted to hear about a young chap who was becoming baseball's favorite character.

Besides being labeled a character and taking an unmerciful riding from the bench jockeys and the newspapermen, Berra wasn't having it all his own way on the diamond. He was a hitter of long-range caliber, but the coaching staff wasn't satisfied with his batting form.

In the field, he was less than satisfactory. Yogi was a clumsy outfielder and a clumsy receiver. He could throw with power but not with accuracy. He could run fast but not always to the right spots. Yankee brass frankly feared he would allow more runs to be scored than he could make with his bat.

Leo Durocher, managing the Dodgers who faced the Yankees in a number of spring training exhibition games, didn't rate Berra too highly at first. "He can hit," Leo said, "what he can reach. Big league curve balls will kill him."

But Durocher learned to respect the little man with the uncanny eye and the outlandish swing, whose booming bat murdered Dodger pitching during the spring training season. Curves didn't curb Yogi's hitting any more than fast balls or pitches over his head or in the dirt.

"I'll be darned," Leo admitted. "I don't know how he does it, but he does it." Durocher shook his head in puzzled admiration. "How do you pitch to a guy like that?"

The Yankees, for their part, never wavered in their feelings. "We'll make a ballplayer out of him," Harris vowed time and again, "if it kills us." Sometimes it seemed it would.

Bucky was impelled by more than Samaritan motives in developing Berra. The Yankees lived and thrived on batting power, both in the American League standings and at the box office. With DiMaggio still nursing a tender heel after his bone spur operation, the Bombers needed bolstering in the clouting department. Yogi looked like the answer.

Where to fit in the graceless Berra was the problem. Bucky had Aaron Robinson and Sherman Lollar for backstop duty. Neither one was great but each was adequate. The best place for Yogi, from a Yankee standpoint, was behind the plate—if only he could catch big league style.

The decision, finally, was to use him as an outfielder. The risk, Bucky and his staff felt, was too great with him receiving, but they had to get Berra's bat into the line-up.

DiMaggio rejoined the team in Washington for the special April 14th opener against the Senators before President Harry S. Truman, but rain postponed the festivities.

Yogi was an eager youngster on the train ride home to New York. Bucky had told him he was starting in right field in the Stadium opener the next day against the Athletics.

The day was bright and clear, with a light breeze that crackled the flags and pennants decorating the vast Yankee ball park. It was Bucky's official debut as the New York manager and crowd of close to forty thousand came to see what sort of a club he had to offer this year.

Phil Marchildon, hurling for the A's, seemed unawed by the Yankee lineup and Yogi Berra in particular. Yogi came up five times without getting a hit, although he smashed a towering fly to deep center which Barney McCoskey barely speared but couldn't get back in time to prevent George McQuinn from scoring after the catch.

Yogi's next appearance came three days later, back in Washington, and this time before the President of the United States. It was an auspicious performance for the boy from The Hill. He whacked out four hits in five times at bat, scored twice and drove in a run as the Yankees walloped the Senators, 7–0.

No one was happy about Berra's work as an outfielder. While he could run with speed, Yogi was slow taking off after the ball. He lacked confidence and judgment on drives. His arm was strong but erratic.

Yogi's awkward meandering in that hallowed area where Babe Ruth once chased fly balls drove Bucky Harris and his staff wild. They tried him as catcher again, then shifted him back to left field. Yogi went willingly and cheerfully, anxious to learn, eager to be of help but just a wee bit lost.

By the end of the 1947 season, he was batting third or fourth and catching most of the time. Neither Robinson nor Lollar, far more proficient receivers, could match his spectacular success at bat.

"You know," Bucky told Coach Frank Crosetti one day, "the kid really has the makings. He's got baseball sense, he can move. I don't know why he can't learn."

"Maybe he's too dumb," someone interjected. "You can't be a catcher without brains."

"Dumb?" Bucky shouted, turning on the speaker. "Let me tell you something," he said, poking his finger into the startled listener's chest, "this kid is dumb as a fox. Uneducated, maybe, and too good natured, but dumb—never!"

That he could think quickly and instinctively was brought forcibly home one day against the St. Louis Browns at the Stadium. A squeeze play was on and Yogi, with pantherish deftness, pounced on the bunt.

With one swift movement, he picked up the ball a few feet in front of the plate and lunged to the right, tagging the batter just under way down the line to first base. Then he plunged sideways to his left to tag the runner coming home from third.

It was an unassisted double play, one of the few in the history of baseball by a catcher. The players made a big joke of it in the clubhouse and Yogi, anxious to be one of the boys, went along with the gag.

"I just got that ball," he told the writers, "and tagged everyone I could see."

"Including the umps?" contributed one jovial scribe.

"Yeah, including the umps."

Rizzuto, dressing near by, slipped Yogi a wink, then murmured to Henrich: "Watch how they twist *that* one!"

A strep throat plagued Berra from midseason on. He had been out of the line-up, suffering from the infection when the team hit St. Louis, where his friends and neighbors from The Hill arranged to celebrate Yogi Berra night at Sportsman's Park.

Waiting for him at home plate was a shower of gifts, donated by the fans, including a new car. The laudatory introductions were over and now the crowd shouted for their hero.

Yogi hunched unhappily in the dugout, frantically memorizing the words typed on a card: "I want to thank everyone who made this night possible."

"C'mon, Yogi," the players yelled, pushing him forward. "Get up there and earn your loot."

Yogi wasn't afraid to stand before seventy thousand people and swing at a ball approaching at one hundred miles an hour, but he was afraid to make a speech. He had read and reread the words on the card at least a thouasnd times. Now it was time to get up and say them.

His face white, his legs quaking, Yogi walked out to home plate and the dreaded microphone. The crowd burst out cheering and he grinned wanly, waving to the many faces which made a white smudge in the glare of the floodlights.

"And now a few words from Yogi himself," he heard the announcer say. Yogi stepped forward, clutched the microphone like a drowning man grasping a life preserver and blurted:

"I want to thank everyone who made this night necessary."

There was a stunned silence for a while, then a huge guffaw as the impact of the words sunk in. Yogi was bewildered at the shrieking laughter, but grateful that his oratorical stint was finished.

He had left a hospital bed in Cleveland to visit St. Louis for the ceremonies, and returned immediately to a local hospital. The strep infection in his throat was so bad he could barely speak.

"Why did you come?" his brother Mike groaned. "It could've been some other night."

"Listen, Mike," Yogi croaked. "These people . . . well, I didn't want to disappoint 'em. I'll be all right."

The Yankees won the pennant running away from the league and Bucky sat down to make World Series plans with his coaches. The Dodgers were practically in as National League champs, so the Yankees knew what they were up against.

"What's the use of kidding?" Frank Crosetti said. "We need Berra's bat."

"Yeah, but the kid's shot full of penicillin," Chuck Dressen pointed out. "He's missed a lot of work the last month."

Finally, the decision was made. Yogi would start the series behind the plate.

"It wouldn't be such a risk," Harris said as the meeting broke up, "if he were in condition. But this way. . . ."

Bucky's concern was not only for the series but also for the promising future of the fantastic little slugger. "If he goes bad in this one," the manager added, "it could ruin him. They'd laugh him out of the league."

Dressen snorted. "Don't worry about Yogi. Nobody'll ever push that bird out of baseball."

"Nope," Bucky said thoughtfully. "He's a tough kid. Just don't forget he's human—a lot more human than you think."

The coaches stared at their boss as he pushed himself heavily from the chair and walked out of the room.

Although it took seven games for the Yankees to defeat the Dodgers for the 1947 World Championship, Yogi Berra seemed to be the lone Yankee who felt no joy in the victory. Many things were troubling him about his performance in the fall classic: only three hits, even though one was the first pinch hit homer in a series game . . . errors . . . bad throws . . . sitting on the bench for the third and fifth games . . . being moved from catcher to right field in the sixth and seventh games. . . . He wondered if he was through as a Yankee and decided the only way to find out was to ask Bucky Harris. Yogi's world was turned right side up again when the manager assured him that they had plans to make him a catcher.

· 6 ·

The day came up gray and cold over St. Louis, but Yogi sighed with pleasure as he studied the familiar drabness of Elizabeth Street from his bedroom window.

It was good to be home. There was comfort in the sounds and the smells of the old house—the wind rattling the windows, the hammer of steam banging through the radiators, the odor of frying peppers drifting up from the kitchen, the drip of the faucet in the bathroom and the way Pop clumped down the steps in the morning.

The anguish of his shattering World Series experience was over. Here on The Hill he was a hero. In fact, Yogi Berra was known anywhere he went in St. Louis. Being with Joey, who was recuperating from a poor season with the Cardinals, had helped, too.

Yogi owned a car now, the one the fans had presented to him, and he and Joey were always driving somewhere around town. Joey had a girl friend, Audrey Ross, on the other side of St. Louis and the three were together a great deal.

There was the gang down at Riva's, the old candy store where the boys hung out, or the Y.M.C.A. where they could see "Uncle" Joe Causino, who had given both boys their start in baseball in their kid days. Or they could drop around to Biggie Garagnano's restaurant for pizza after the St. Louis Flyers' hockey games.

Hockey. Now that was fun. Yogi pressed his forehead against the windowpane, savoring the cold flatness against his skin, remembering the night he and Joey dressed in hockey regalia and posed for pictures on the arena ice.

They hadn't played, of course. "Wotta pair of bums we are," Yogi sputtered between choked laughs as he and Joey slid, wobbled and slipped on the ice. The pictures were real cute. The best one showed Yogi sprawled on the ice in front of the goal, pretending he was stopping the puck.

Boy, the furore in the Yankee office when Red Patterson, the publicity director, spotted the pictures in a New York newspaper! "Suppose you got hit in the eye, Yogi!" Patterson wailed over the long-distance wires.

It was easy to promise that he wouldn't put on ice skates again. He didn't give a hoot about playing hockey but it was very flattering to learn that the Yankees were so concerned about his well-being.

"They're like my own family," Yogi told Joey with grave innocence.

Garagiola rolled his eyes skyward and ignored the remark. "Let's play some handball down at the Y."

After the workout they drifted over to Biggie's restaurant for a snack. Yogi noticed a petite, strikingly pretty waitress on the other side of the restaurant. She had a trim figure, dark blond hair and a vivacious manner.

"Gee, I'd like to meet a girl like that," he said, nodding in the waitress' direction.

"Why a girl like that?" grinned Joey. "Why not *that* girl?"

"I dunno," Yogi balked. "She's not waiting on us. Say, you think I can meet her?"

Joey patted his friend's head gently as he arose. "In

these matters of the heart, m'lord," he said, bowing slightly, "leave it to your true and trusted servant. . . ."

"Hey, wait," Yogi clutched Joey's sleeve. "You can't go over like that. . . ."

"Tut, tut, Sir Gawain," Garagiola said, gently disengaging Berra's hold. "There are ways and ways. Watch me."

Joey caught the owner's eye and beckoned him over. Wearing a grin almost as enormous as his cigar, Biggie bustled across.

"My good pal here of the New York Yankees, champeens of the world," Joey explained, "would like to meet yon damsel in the blue uniform." He pointed to the waitress.

"Oh, oh," Biggie said. "Carmen Short. I don't know if she likes baseball players." He looked soberly at Yogi, surreptitiously nudging Garagiola. "But maybe—"

"Yeah," Joey picked it up. "The way he plays, maybe she won't consider him a ballplayer."

Biggie laughed and walked over to Carmen. Yogi nervously watched their pantomime through the noise and bustle of the busy restaurant during the lunch hour. Then the proprietor turned back to them.

His face was grave. "I tried," he shrugged. "She says she won't go out with a married man."

"Married man!" Yogi exploded. "Biggie, I'm a bachelor all my life! What is this, a gag?"

"Sure, that's what I told her," the restaurateur agreed. "But she thinks you're Terry Moore and she read that he's married."

"Terry Moore's with the Cards," Yogi shouted, indignation on his face. Then, despairingly: "I guess that's really the brush-off, isn't it?"

Biggie couldn't stand the "hurt puppy" expression. "Naw," he laughed. "It's all right. I convinced her you're not that good. You're not Terry Moore. She'll meet you later."

They went out on a double date with Joe and Audrey to a hockey game and after that Yogi saw Carmen regularly. It was love all right, and Yogi was thinking of marriage before he left for spring training in sunny St. Petersburg in February.

In his own bashful way, he managed to get things done. Carmen was on her lunch hour in the restaurant when Yogi ambled in and sat down next to her.

After some small talk, he stumbled into a strange silence, staring at her as she ate. Then, almost hypnotically, he reached into his jacket pocket, slowly withdrew a small box and slid it across the table in front of her.

Carmen paused, knife and fork in mid-air. Neither uttered a word, gazing at each other in rapt silence.

She wiped her fingers daintily on a napkin, then reached for the box and opened it. Inside nestled a large, glittering diamond engagement ring. Yogi studied her, fear and hope written on his face.

"It's beautiful," Carmen murmured, her cheeks pale and her lips trembling. "It's beautiful. . . ." Then she slipped it on her finger.

Yogi's eyes danced. Cautiously he pushed his hand toward hers and held it tightly. He couldn't say what was choked up inside him, but she understood.

Pressing his hand, looking at him through a teary mist, Carmen said simply: "I love you, Yogi."

Berra arrived at the Yankee training camp in St. Petersburg in the spring of 1948 with a joyous heart. It was a balmy spring, golden with sunshine; Carmen loved him; he was a Yankee. What more could a young man want from life?

His first glimpse of the practice diamond, set like a clay-red jewel in a sea of gleaming emerald, stirred a yearning for action which he had never imagined he could feel.

"Take it easy," Yogi was warned as, like a child turned loose in a candy factory, he rushed around with frenzied eagerness. He radiated an enthusiasm and sheer delight which infected everyone on the field.

"Look at that kid," remarked Eddie Dyer, the Cardinals' manager, as Yogie bounced around the diamond. "You'd never think he had a miserable World Series."

The Redbirds worked out with the Yankees and Dyer was standing on the side talking to a newspaperman. "He's just happy to be in a monkey suit. But take my boy"—nodding his head toward Joe Garagiola warming up a pitcher—"he's still brooding over last season."

"They're pals, from the same neighborhood, the same street. You figure they should be the same. But Joe worries and Yogi laughs." Eddie sighed. "I wish Garagiola could forget about last year. He could be a great catcher if he'd let himself."

The newspaperman ambled over to Bucky Harris on the other side of the field. "I'm glad it's Eddie who has the worrier," the Yankee pilot grinned, "and not me. Anyway, some of those steals by the Dodgers weren't Berra's fault. The pitchers let those fellows get too much of a jump."

Several other sports writers drifted over. "Bucky," asked one, "does that mean you're sticking with Yogi as a catcher?"

"Why not?" the manager argued. "I think he can be a good receiver and I know he's a good hitter. Look, I traded Aaron Robinson to the White Sox, didn't I?"

Someone snickered. "Sure, but you still have three other catchers besides Berra." The scoffer meant Sherman Lollar, Gus Niarhos and Charlie Silvera.

Bucky smiled knowingly. "Who's out there catching now?" he asked. His listeners glanced automatically toward the diamond, where Berra crouched behind the plate in a "hi-lo" drill with Coach Charlie Dressen.

Each day at the end of regular practice, Yogi and Chuck spent thirty minutes in the arduous, back-breaking drill they called "hi-lo." Standing in the batter's box, Dressen bunted the ball to the right of the plate. Yogi pounced on it in a few quick strides, straightened up and snapped it back to the coach. Then Dressen plunked it down the third base line and Yogi would be on it again. The drill continued endlessly.

"It puts the cat in a catcher," Bucky explained, his eyes following the punishing exercise. "We're doing other things with him. Throwing, receiving. . . . Trouble is that this game means only one thing to him . . . hitting. But he'll learn."

There was the annoying snicker again and the Yankee manager grimaced. "He is learning, all right. Yogi *can* throw but he doesn't know how. He knows what pitches should be called, but he doesn't know when. Experience will take care of that."

Harris left to confer with his infielders and one writer shook his head sadly. "What a letdown he's in for. That kid'll never be a big league catcher."

Through for the day, Yogi trudged across the diamond, lugging his catching paraphernalia.

"Hey, Yogi," one of the writers called. Berra turned politely. "Bucky says you're his regular catcher."

Yoki ducked his head with a smile. He was getting on to these newspapermen. The trick was to be pleasant, say enough but not too much.

"I'm a lucky guy to play anywhere on this club," he said

after a pause. "But I'd rather play one position than shift around from catcher to outfielder like I did last year."

Speaking now, he realized it was a thought he had never expressed before. Last season he had been a confused, frightened rookie, shunting back and forth between two completely unrelated positions. Maybe this year, sticking to one job, he could master it.

His hitting, Berra knew, would improve. He had tried to pull too many pitches to right field and the hurlers quickly got on to him. His batting average perked up when he started slicing the outside deliveries to left field.

With Bucky Harris, Chuck Dressen, Johnny Schulte and Paul Krichell working on him daily, Yogi discovered more about baseball than he knew existed. Conversely, his teachers discovered that he absorbed more than they had anticipated.

Yogi's training halted temporarily when he sprained his foot sliding into third base in a game with the Phillies in Clearwater on March 15th. Until Dr. Sidney Gaynor, the team physician, examined him, it was feared he had broken an ankle, so intense was the pain.

"How is it, Doc?" a worried Harris asked.

"I think it's just a sprain," the doctor answered solemnly. This his eyes brightened. "Know what he asked me out there when I thought I'd have to give him a shot because of the pain? He wanted to know if he'd be able to go to the movies tonight!"

It was a bad break for the kid, the manager thought, coming just when he had begun to show real spark as a catcher. Only two days before, Yogi had taken the cockiness out of the Cardinals, who boasted they would run the bases at will on him.

It was the Yankees' second exhibition game of the season with the Redbirds and Red Embree was pitching, with

Berra behind the plate. The Cards were giving Yogi a real ride from the bench, harping on his inept throwing in the 1947 series.

Embree walked Erv Dusak, the lead-off man, and Terry Moore came up to bat. On the first pitch, Dusak scooted for second base but found the ball waiting in George Stirnweiss' glove for an easy out. Berra had pegged it perfectly.

"Lucky, lucky," the bench jockeys hooted. Yogi merely grinned. Moore walked and when Stan Musial swung at a third strike, Terry made his dash for second. Again the ball was waiting, this time in Gerry Coleman's hands. The throw was so good that Moore didn't attempt a slide.

"What's with this guy?" one of the Cards players asked Garagiola.

"Don't underrate him," Joey warned. "You don't know how good Yogi is."

Whether they did or not, the Cardinals didn't try to steal on him again. Neither did anyone laugh at the pump-shaped Berra when he stepped into the batter's box. His eye and his power were too formidable.

"That's a real pro swing," Stan Musial, one of the great hitters of baseball, said from the dugout. "See the wrist snap he gets into it."

Garagiola brought Moore over after the game. "Meet the man who almost ruined your love life," he quipped, introducing the tall, grinning St. Louis outfielder.

Walking out together, Moore praised Yogi's throwing. "You sure cooked our goose fast," he chuckled.

"He would've done the same in the series, too," Garagiola said loyally. "Yogi was punch-drunk with penicillin. He got more needles in him than a porcupine."

Yogi laughed. Next to Groucho Marx, Joey was the funniest man in the world to him. But he didn't want excuses for his lame throwing in the 1947 series. The fact was that now he did throw to the bases better.

Bucky Harris and his crew had corrected several faults. Instead of bobbing out of a crouch with his feet crossed in the old Berra fashion, Yogi now pegged from an erect, relaxed position. He got the ball away faster and with more control.

Yogi remembered the talk he had with Bucky Harris the second day of spring training. They were sitting near the water bucket. He had run several laps around the field and slumped limply to the bench, panting and spent. The manager plopped down beside him.

"We'll start working on your throwing tomorrow," Harris said, squinting into the flattened rays of the sinking sun. Yogi said nothing, but his heart sank.

"I've seen a lot of young fellows with the same faults," the pilot continued. "I know because I had the same ones. I was wild as a March hare when I came up." He paused reflectively, remembering his early shortstop days.

"When I let go of the ball I never was sure whether it would stop at first base or wind up in the grandstand. You see, I did what you do now."

Yogi was all ears, his exhaustion forgotten.

"I took too long getting the ball away," Harris said, "and then I had to put so much stuff on it, my accuracy was off." He watched Berra squirm into a more comfortable position.

"Yeah," Yogi grunted. "I see what you mean. But . . . I dunno, sometimes I think it's my fingers. . . ."

Bucky's brows came down in a puzzled frown.

"They're too short," Yogi finished, holding up his hands. His eyes held a mute appeal which touched Harris.

"No, Yogi," he smiled. "It's not the size of your fingers. It's what you do with them. Your arm is stronger than mine and I got to be a pretty good chucker by working on it."

He rose, patting Berra's shoulder. "You work on it, you'll be all right."

The manager strolled off leaving Yogi sprawled motionless across the hard bench with a faraway look in his eyes. I'll try, he promised himself. I'll really try.

· 7 ·

The 1948 season was not a roaring success for Berra, the Yankees or for Manager Bucky Harris.

Yogi's greenness showed pitifully through the thin veneer of experience he had already acquired in the major leagues. His catching left a great deal to be desired and his hitting, while powerful and at times awesome, suffered its low moments.

He started poorly with the bat, remaining under or around the .250 mark for the better part of two months, then climbed slowly to .271 by August 14th when Harris shifted him to the outfield and stuck Gus Niarhos behind the plate.

As Milt Gross, the noted sports columnist who covered the Yankees that year, wrote in the New York *Post*, ". . . as a catcher, Yogi not only was a hindrance to the defense and his own hitting, but also to the pitchers, who had little influence on him. There is also the suspicion held by some of the Yankees better thinkers that Yogi, living in constant dread and fear of base-stealing forays against him, signaled for fast balls to get the drop on runners when the situation clearly called for curve balls."

But there were also flashes of near-brilliance when Yogi handled his receiving chores with aplomb and finesse.

There was a game, for instance, in June against the Cleveland Indians at the Stadium in which he made six superb fielding plays, including three perfect pegs to second base to nip attempted steals.

It annoyed him when a pitcher shook off his signal. He felt it showed lack of confidence in his judgment, but the Yankees regarded it more logically. They placed more faith in their more experienced hurlers than in Berra, particularly in tight situations.

Harris realized how important confidence—the feeling of security and belonging—was to Berra. Whenever possible, he and the Yankee coaches went out of their way to praise Yogi's work. They watched over him off the field as well as on it.

Once before a game, Johnny Lindell and a particularly opinionated newspaperman got into a friendly but heated clubhouse argument. Both were making their points forcibly, unaware of a most rapt listener, until Yogi suddenly barged in. He repeated Lindell's arguments almost word for word, even mimicking Lindell's speech and mannerisms. For some reason Yogi's intrusion, his aping of Lindell and his unfamiliarity with the topic under discussion, infuriated the reporter who turned on Berra and snapped: "Stop acting like a busher and imitating grown men."

Yogi paled and stepped back, stuttering apologetically, then fled. Lindell stood aghast, sorry for his young teammate but helpless to repair the damage.

Fifteen minutes later the newspaperman was asked to join Harris in his office. Bucky was pleasant but serious.

"I understand you had some sort of a run-in with Yogi," he said. The reporter, the chip still on his shoulder, sailed into Bucky too. He let the manager know that his discussion with Lindell wasn't Yogi's business and that his words with Berra weren't Harris' concern.

"Okay, okay," Harris agreed. "I'm not interfering with what you want to say to any of my ballplayers. But I wish you would do me a favor."

Bucky possessed strong charm and a flattering manner. He gave the writer a man-of-the-world smile. "You know how Yogi is," he said with a lift of his eyebrows. "There isn't a drop of meanness in him. The kid wants to be accepted, to be part of the group, to be like the other fellows. You know, talk like them, act like them. . . . I guess he was trying to be one of the boys when he stuck his nose in where it didn't belong."

The writer, mollified and slightly ashamed of his short temper with Berra, nodded agreeably.

"Calling him a busher must have hurt. Maybe he is one now, but it won't be forever. You could help both Yogi and me if you would find an opportunity to tell him he really isn't bush, that you were angry and lost your temper. . . . You know what I mean."

"If you think it'll help, Bucky . . . ," the writer shrugged.

"I do, very much. He's the kind of kid who'll believe he's good if he's told it over and over again."

Bucky clapped his hand on the writer's shoulder and grinned. "I told him you didn't mean it. I wish you would, too."

It was part of a subtle campaign waged all that year to instill confidence in the young slugger. One day at Briggs Stadium in Detroit before a game with the Tigers, Bucky halted Yogi.

"This park is made for a hitter like you," the manager said, motioning toward the right field stands only three hundred and twenty-five feet from home plate. "I don't see how you can miss hitting homers here."

A couple of newspapermen, sitting with Bucky, chuckled after Berra left, eyes alight and face beaming.

"Who do you think you are—Svengali?" one of them joked. Bucky's only response was a polite smile.

It became a smug smile when Berra won the game for the Yankees with a home run blast into the right field sector in the ninth inning.

Yogi sought out the scribes in the clubhouse after the game. "Hey, this must be my park, all right," he said with a wise wag of his head.

When the Yankees next met the Tigers, it was in the Stadium. Bucky pulled Berra aside. "Remember, this team is your meat," he said.

Apparently, the difference in ball parks never occurred to Yogi, who hammered another homer that day.

Bucky seldom missed an opportunity to bolster Berra's morale as batter or catcher. Once in Boston, with Ted Williams of the Red Sox at bat and Joe Page on the mound, the left-handed pitcher shook off Yogi's call.

Page sent in a blazing fast ball, letter high, which Ted poked into the bleachers for a homer. Berra had signaled for a curve inside and the entire dugout knew it.

Bucky jabbed Yogi in the ribs after the inning. "Maybe that'll teach some of these smart pitchers to listen to Yogi," he said with a broad wink.

But Harris couldn't bamboozle Berra into being the catcher he needed as the Yankees trailed the Cleveland Indians in the American League pennant race. By mid-August, Bucky was desperate.

Shifting Berra to the outfield kept his bat in the game and another strong stick was added at first base, where right fielder Tommy Henrich replaced lighter-hitting George McQuinn.

The move worked like magic for a while. With Yogi rambling the outfield and suddenly walloping the ball at a .400 pace, the Yankees won fifteen of their next eighteen games. Berra's war club hammered out thirty-four hits in that stretch, including three homers, four triples and five doubles.

Yogi was happy over the change. Not only did it remove the burden of catching but it took him away from the snipers in the enemy dugout and the stands.

As an outfielder, he didn't trample Joe DiMaggio, who flanked him in center, or run into the fences as had been predicted. He was guilty of no mental lapses, followed the game intelligently and didn't throw wild even if he wasn't a polished fly chaser.

Berra felt his hitting was helped by not having to squat behind the plate in heavy catching equipment. "On hot days when you're catching," he told Phil Rizzuto, "the bat gets real heavy after you've been up a couple of times."

The Scooter confessed to being puzzled at why Berra hit at so many bad balls. "I still get plenty of good hits, don't I?" Yogi retorted amiably.

"It's a habit, maybe, just like my always hitting the first ball. If it's good—good for me, anyway—why pass it up? The pitchers are always looking to get ahead of you and I like to get that first one in."

Carmen, with whom he corresponded almost daily, came to see him play when the Yankees were in St. Louis. The cruel taunts of the bench jockeys aggravated her.

"They don't bother me," Yogi assured her. "I just laugh at them. The White Sox are toughest on me and the A's do a pretty good job."

"What do they say?" she asked, concern in her lovely dark eyes.

Yogi reddened. "I don't like to say what they call me."

He didn't tell her about that day in Boston in 1947, his first year in the majors, and his introduction to Fenway

Park. A Boston Red Sox coach stopped him on the dugout steps.

"You all right, kid?" the veteran asked.

"Sure," Yogi answered, flattered at the attention. "I feel fine."

"That's funny," the Bostonian said with mock concern. "Nobody could look that bad without being sick."

Yogi was anxious to please. "Well, my stomach was a bit off this morning. . . ."

"No, not your belly," the ribber continued. "Your face. I never saw an uglier one."

Yogi didn't lose his temper. His frown turned into a naïve, trusting mask as he replied: "So I'm ugly. In this racket all you gotta do is hit the ball—and you don't do it with your face!"

It had hurt then. Now it didn't mean a thing. If anyone as beautiful as Carmen could be engaged to him, then being ugly wasn't the worst thing in the world.

His brothers Tony and Mike were at the game with Carmen. Now they were driving back to The Hill with Yogi for an evening with the folks, and the first gush of chatter was over.

Tony broke the silence. "You throw good from the outfield," he said. "You've got the arm. Why can't you throw to second when you're catching?"

Yogi thought for a while. "The trouble is that when I'm catching and there's a man on, I start thinking. . . . You know, like I better make it good . . . something like that. I think about it so much I get tense. When I was in the minors I never thought about it. I dared them to run on me."

His growing uncertainty as a receiver was the main reason for Yogi's switch to the outfield. Of all things, Bucky Harris didn't want Berra to lose confidence in himself. The manager had spent too much time building up the young man's ego to risk tearing it down before the job was completed.

"The way he bats," Bucky told a friend, "Berra has to be in the line-up. He'll be a catcher someday, but meanwhile he can play out there . . . just as long as he gets his licks up at bat."

The Yankees finished third in the 1948 campaign. Spurred by the brash Lou Boudreau, Cleveland won the American League pennant and beat the Boston Braves, four games to two, in the World Series. Yogi wound up with a .305 batting average which included one hundred and forty-three hits. He clouted fourteen homers, ten triples and twenty-four doubles.

Significantly, he drove in ninety-eight runs in his one hundred and twenty-five games, topped only by DiMaggio and Henrich. He had been deadly in the pinches, a batter who could deliver with men on base, the hallmark of an outstanding hitter.

When the season ended, Yogi rushed back to St. Louis and Carmen. Joe Garagiola was back, too, a disappointed and bewildered young man. The home town fans had turned on him during his slump, ridiculing and abusing him to the point where he no longer could play effectively.

It was a curious contrast to the previous year. By unspoken agreement, these two close friends did not discuss baseball. Yogi was busy with arrangements for his marriage in January. Joey was to be best man.

One of the new Berra stories which began to circulate as the wedding approached was supposed to have happened in downtown St. Louis. Yogi, the anecdote went, bumped into Pete Reiser of the Boston Braves.

"Are ya coming to my wedding?" Berra asked.

Pete grinned and nodded. "Sure am, Yogi boy."

"Okay, then," Berra said, digging into his pocket and coming out with an engraved invitation. "No sense wasting an invite if you weren't coming."

It wasn't true, of course, but served to irritate Carmen considerably. To her, Yogi was a sweet, trusting chap, so completely guileless and good natured that he would never deny these anecdotes of his own volition. She was distressed at the tendency to ridicule him.

"Why do they do that to Yogi?" she asked Garagiola one evening. "He doesn't say one tenth of what they attribute to him. When he's with the fellows they do all the talking and he does all the laughing."

Joey's answer was simple. "They do it because they like him. They really do . . . the fans, the players . . . everyone. Because they laugh doesn't mean they don't respect him. Don't ever forget that."

Carmen and Yogi were married in St. Ambrose Church in a formal affair with all the trimmings, and spent their honeymoon in Florida. A baseball pal kidded the ugly Yogi about snaring such an attractive wife. The snapback was quick and to the point: "I'm human, ain't I?"

At a sports banquet that winter, Yogi was interviewed by Harry Caray, who broadcast the St. Louis Cardinals games.

"How did you manage to marry a girl named Carmen Short? That's not an Italian name? I'll bet the girls on The Hill aren't happy about that!"

Yogi had the answer out faster than a throw to second base. "They had their chance," he grinned, evoking an appreciative roar from the crowd.

· 8 ·

It was late afternoon in the early spring of 1949, blazing
hot under a sun that hung like yellow flame in the bright
blue skies above St. Petersburg, Florida.

Yogi squatted wearily into catching position for the thousandth time that day, his uniform drenched and his face
speckled with globules of sweat. His hand floated with
moisture inside the mitt, his knees ached and his back was
a mass of taut, screaming muscles.

The pitcher threw the ball and Yogi waited, rising
slightly in his crouch close to the plate, right foot a few
inches farther back than his left. The ball smacked into
his mitt and he was up and forward in one motion, right
hand cocked for the throw, body in perfect balance.

"Good. That's it." The words came in a pleasant drawl
from a strapping, long-legged man with a powerful build
and the leathery good looks of an outdoor man. This was
Bill Dickey, the greatest receiver in Yankee history, now
back with the club as a coach.

Big, genial Bill was home with his Yankees again after
two years' absence while Bucky Harris managed the team.
Bucky was gone now and Casey Stengel became the new
pilot. Casey, the comedian, the man with the knowing
eyes and caustic wit who had been a star outfielder for the

New York Giants from 1912 to 1925 and a National League manager from 1934 to 1943, always with second division clubs.

Stengel's first move was to hire Dickey, not only for his all-round baseball knowledge that made him a priceless asset as coach, but for what he could do with the raw but powerful Berra.

Dickey knew all there was to know about the art of receiving. He had been a superlative hitter, too. In nineteen seasons as a Yankee, Big Bill had compiled a .313 lifetime batting average. He had caught in thirty-eight World Series games and eight All-Star contests. He was wise, patient, articulate—a perfect teacher.

Their first day down at St. Petersburg, Casey studied Berra with a puzzled look. Head cocked birdlike, shoulders hunched, Casey watched Yogi frolic around the diamond. "What do you make of him, Bill?" he asked.

Dickey was silent for a moment. "He's got something," the lanky former catcher said slowly. "The kid's strong and he can move . . . good co-ordination, too," he added. "I've seen him powder the ball."

Casey gave him a quizzical look. "Can he catch?"

Dickey hesitated. "Not yet," he said finally.

"Does that mean . . . ?" Casey tugged his lower lip and waited for the answer.

"Yeah, Case, it does," Bill said, nodding. "I think he can do it, physically. Whether he wants to be a catcher badly enough to learn all over again is a different matter. We'll find that out soon."

It was an astute observation. Yogi, who had loved working behind the plate in his sand lot and minor league days, was chary of it now. His confidence gone, he felt uncomfortable and unhappy catching, and the worry interfered with his hitting. However, winding up the 1948 campaign as a relatively carefree outfielder had lifted his average considerably.

Yogi realized that the Yankees were paying him for what he did with the stick, not the glove. Why else would they have yielded to his holdout demands and raised his contract salary from eighty-five hundred dollars to twelve thousand, five hundred?

He had held out for three weeks, stubbornly insisting on a pay hike. It had been a pleasant siege for him, honeymooning with Carmen in Florida, but not so happy for General Manager George Weiss.

"I had a good year in 1948," Berra argued. "I drove in ninety-eight runs. Only two other guys beat me out and they get a lot more dough than I do. I'm married now. I got responsibilities back home in St. Louis, too. I'm lucky to be a Yankee, sure. But the Yankees ain't exactly suffering from smallpox because they got me around."

Yogi remained firm until Weiss finally capitulated, whereupon the catcher sailed into his work with wholehearted glee.

Dickey approached his task realistically. Berra looked clumsy, but he was quick and agile. He could get off fast, caught the ball well and had baseball instinct. "If you have that," Bill told his pupil, "all you have to do is practice and the rest comes naturally. It took me six years to become a first-class catcher."

He cornered Berra before practice one morning. It was a delightful spring day, the air soft and exhilarating.

"Yogi, what position do you want to play?"

"Makes no difference to me," Berra answered quickly—maybe too quickly. "All I want to be sure is that I play." He paused to pick up a bat and test its weight in his wide hands. "A baseball player's got to be in there every day if he wants to get the cash."

"Is that what you like most about baseball—money?"

Yogi hated to sound like a softie, but he had to be truthful. "Nope. I guess it ain't."

"Well, what is?" Dickey persisted.

Yogi gave it sober thought. "Hitting," he said. "I enjoy that most."

Dickey had suspected it. As long as Berra thought swinging a bat was the entire game of baseball, he never would become a good catcher. It was this wrong thinking of Yogi's which Bill had to change.

"Then I suppose you don't care about catching," Dickey said.

"Yes, I do." Berra sounded hurt.

"But you'd rather play the outfield. You think it's a softer job . . . just standing out there in between times at bat. Is that it?"

A worried frown creased Yogi's forehead as he listened.

Dickey continued. "You may as well know now that if you want to stick it out as an outfielder, you'll have to put in a lot of work, too."

So began Berra's education in the intricacies of big league catching. Dickey worked, taught, coaxed, demonstrated—all with patience and forbearance.

Converting Berra from a liability behind the plate to a first-class backstop was a monotonous, wearying task. Yogi would be the key player, the man who had to handle every pitch, throw to the bases, handle bunts, grab pop fouls, do the heavy thinking on the field.

It was a wonderful and enlightening period for Yogi. He was given insight into baseball subtleties and arts of which he had never dreamed. "That Dickey!" he told Phil Rizzuto. "He knows everything. And he's teaching me all his experiences!"

Dickey did not act the martinet. His criticisms were

couched gently as suggestions. His voice was soft, his manner always warm. He was generous with praise, mindful always of the deep inner sensitivity Yogi carefully hid from the world.

Gradually, Berra responded to Bill's coaching. "The kid is really trying," Dickey told Stengel. "He's gonna make it, Case."

They sat for a while watching Berra work in an infield drill.

"Look at his stance behind the plate," Dickey pointed out. "He used to throw off balance. I don't doubt that he was pegging curves down to second. It's a wonder he didn't throw outdrops."

Stengel seemed pleased. "He sets himself pretty good now."

"This way," Dickey added, "Yogi's in better position to move . . . to throw, pick up a bunt or go after a pop foul."

Batting practice started and Berra tugged his mask on and crouched behind the plate. He kept up a steady stream of chatter with the batters.

"Perky kid," Stengel commented with an amused gleam.

"It's confidence," Dickey said. "He's getting to feel like a catcher."

The manager's approving nod was like sunshine to Dickey.

"He's playing up closer to the plate now," Dickey went on. "He was too far away before. Many catchers stand too far back because they think they'll be hit by the bat. Actually, when you're up close there's less danger from foul tips. Those mean slices whistle past instead of hitting you in the arms or legs."

Bill recalled how quickly Berra had grasped the lesson

on footwork. He had put George Stirnweiss on second base and ordered the catcher to throw to him.

"By staying closer to the plate," Dickey said, demonstrating, "you can step entirely over home plate in firing the ball." He shot a strike to Stirnweiss.

"You've got to step over it in making the throw," he explained to the attentive Berra. "Get used to doing that and the throw becomes automatic. Soon you'll know just how hard and high to throw each time."

He made Yogi try it several times and the improvement was readily apparent.

"That's why so many guys have been trying to steal on you," Dickey said. "A catcher who stands back an extra foot or two invites steals."

Yogi nodded vigorously. "Sure, I know why," he said excitedly. "The ball takes longer to get to you. If it's a curve or a sailer, it's even worse and you're out of position."

Dickey noticed the eagerness, the new enthusiasm lighting up his pupil, and felt pleased.

"I got it now," Yogi almost shouted, banging his fist into the mitt. "Wait'll I get those guys now. . . ."

Dickey taught him how to go after pop flies properly. "That's no problem once you learn how to watch the ball leaving the bat. Just start in the same direction the ball takes, look up—and there it is."

He showed the neophyte how to grip the ball properly. Dickey felt part of Yogi's trouble with the throw was his anxiety to get the ball away.

"Yogi, you hurry too much," he said. "You see the runner start and you can't wait to get the ball. The result is that you have no control over it. It's just as easy to get a good grip as to fumble around with it when it finally comes in."

Dickey showed Yogi how to trap low balls in front of the

plate, how to shift with the ball, how to run back for a high foul behind the plate—all the fine points of backstopping.

Equally important, Dickey awakened Berra's pride in himself and his catching. Stengel and the other coaches joined him in doing everything they could to build Yogi's ego.

"There aren't many good catchers," Dickey said one day as they relaxed in the dugout. Early dusk crept across the field like a violet shadow. They were alone, the last two off the field after a taxing drill.

"It's a tough position," he continued, resting against the damp wall. "Once you've established yourself, you've got a job for years."

He let that sink in. "You've got a big advantage over fellows who are just receivers. You can hit. That's why you're in this league. I can't teach you to hit but I can help you become a catcher. You've got to help yourself improve, too."

They sat in silence for a while, each lost in his own thoughts.

Yogi spoke first. "Is that how it was with you?" he asked timidly.

Dickey nodded. "Not exactly. You see, Yogi, I always wanted to be a catcher. Nothing else. I practiced constantly when I was a kid."

He paused reflectively, remembering his hard struggle up through the minor leagues.

"Some fellows say they'd never want to catch; it's too tough. Me . . . I loved it."

He turned to Yogi. "I think you will, too. Baseball is in your blood. Catching is where all the excitement and action and thinking is."

Berra's surprised look didn't escape him.

"Yeah, I said thinking," he repeated with extra force.

"You can outthink most of these guys out there in monkey suits. Sure, you read comic books and the boys play jokes on you and you do get off some funny cracks ... but that doesn't make you a dope."

Berra's eyes widened incredulously. His tongue stuck in his mouth with embarrassment and a tiny thrill of gratification rippled through him.

"I've watched you, Yogi," Dickey drawled matter-of-factly. "You make the instinctive move. You have a feel for catching ... something that tells you what a batter's weaknesses and strengths are. I like the way you handle pitchers, the way they like you and relax."

It was growing dark and slightly cool. Dickey straightened up. "C'mon, let's get into the showers." They got up and walked into the clubhouse, Yogi more thoughtful than usual.

They were alone in the dressing room toweling briskly when Yogi spoke again.

"Yeah, Bill," he said as though in revelation, "I like catching ... you know, like you do."

He looked at Dickey, who smiled but remained silent.

They finished dressing and strolled out to the parking lot, their silence almost a form of communication, a sign somehow that they were synchronized in thought and feeling.

Dickey climbed into his car, started the motor and looked up. Yogi was standing alongside with a wistful expression.

"Bill—" He started, then hesitated. "Do you think I can make it—as a catcher, I mean?"

"If I didn't think so," Dickey answered, "I wouldn't be here."

It was the truth and it sent Berra home to his honeymoon beach bungalow an exultant young man.

But Dickey knew how far Yogi still was from being the

polished, valuable backstop the Yankees needed. Learning and trying in practice was one thing; doing it effectively in competition was another.

Still, he had the feeling this kid would make the grade. Stengel had said the big thing was to get Berra to believe in himself, that the rest would follow.

"Well," Dickey mused grimly as he tooled his car expertly along the highway, "we've convinced Berra that he's a catcher. Now let's see if he can convince us."

· 9 ·

The motor purred like a tiger kitten, powerful but pleasant, as Yogi let his car out a bit on the Florida highway leading to the Yankee training camp at St. Petersburg.

The morning was bright and clear, the smooth road empty for miles ahead. Yogi's eyes and reflexes automatically tended to the driving chores. In his mind, he was swinging a bat and running around the bases on the ball field.

The radio blared a popular song and the sun warmed his left arm resting on the window ledge of the car door. He sighed in contentment, at peace with himself and the world. Suddenly, from the corner of his eye, he became aware of movement on the seat next to him.

It was a bottle of shampoo rolling about on the seat. Yogi had wanted to wash his hair in the showers after practice and asked Carmen to get him a special soap lotion he favored. He had put it down next to him and forgotten it.

Now it rolled up and almost over the edge of the seat, then back and forward again. Yogi slowed the car slightly, glanced quickly at the road ahead and up at his rear window mirror to make sure no cars were close, then reached over for the bottle.

It rolled away like a playful puppy teasing its master. He stretched over farther, his left hand dragging imperceptibly on the steering wheel. Then, too late, he saw the palm tree looming before him and slammed on the brake just before the car struck.

For a moment he sat stunned and frightened after the crunching impact. The sound of the motor ceased but the radio still played. An announcer gaily spieled his glib but spurious commercial on a breakfast cereal.

Yogi looked around, surprised. The car was diagonally off the road, driven right into a giant palm tree. His knee hurt but otherwise he felt intact. Gingerly, he opened the door and got out of the car.

He moved his arms and legs, flexed his muscles. Nothing really hurt. His knee was slightly cut and his trousers torn. The car didn't fare as well, however. The radiator grille was ruined. Yogi surveyed it glumly, then brightened momentarily. Still clutched in his right hand, unbroken, was the bottle of shampoo!

Casey Stengel and the rest of the Yankee management breathed easier at Yogi's escape from personal damage. With Joe DiMaggio's heel apt to keep him out of action for months yet and Charlie Keller ailing, the Bombers needed Berra's bat desperately.

Yogi had his minor miseries during the training and exhibition game program. He banged up his hands several times and injured his side in a crack-up at the plate. But his play in general delighted Stengel and his staff.

It was Gus Niarhos, however, not Berra, who caught the 1949 season opener against the Washington Senators. Yogi had the sniffles and a slight fever. Stengel, harassed by what would develop into a record campaign for Yankee injuries, was taking no chances.

DiMaggio was off his crutches at last, but there still was

no telling how long it would be before Jolting Joe returned to action. It was a close game and Casey had to call on Yogi before it was won, 3–2.

Phil Rizzuto had reached second base on a walk and a sacrifice when Stengel told Yogi to grab a bat. It was two out in the eighth inning and the score tied, 2–2. The Bombers hadn't done much against Sid Hudson, the tall Washington right-hander.

Yogi idly swung two bats as he strode slowly to the plate. There were some scattered hoots from the stands and the Senators' dugout, but he was oblivious to them. He tossed his warm-up bat away, settled into a comfortable stance and waited for the pitch.

Hudson poured one inside for a ball. Yogi was tempted to swing, but remembered Casey's warning: "Don't take the first pitch, feller, even if it's big and fat and right over the plate."

Every pitcher in the league, Stengel pointed out, knew Berra was a first-ball hitter. "So you'll never get a decent one to hit," Casey lectured. "All you need is one good one to hit, and the pitcher's gotta come in with it sometime if you wait him out."

"Yeah," Yogi agreed, "but what if he don't?"

Casey snorted. "So you walk. That's a man on base for us and no time at bat for you." He poked Yogi and winked. Yogi regarded him blankly.

"Don't you see?" Stengel resumed. "Last year you batted .305 with one hundred and forty-three hits. You got only twenty-five walks. Suppose you got thirty more passes."

He paused to relish the curiosity in Berra's gaze.

"You know what average that'd give you?"

Casey didn't wait for an answer. "Twenty points more," he said, raising his voice. "You'd have hit .325!"

Yogi's mind grasped the logic of his manager's words,

but his instincts couldn't keep him from swinging. The pitch might look bad to others, but *he* saw it.

"What's the matter, Berra," the Washington catcher asked as Yogi dug in for the next pitch, "was that one too good for you?"

Hudson's next try barely skimmed the dirt outside and the catcher dove to stop it. Yogi glanced over to the dugout and Stengel nodded. The sign was still on to hit.

Yogi bit at the next one, a fast curve that just curled off his bat into the stands behind him. Two balls, one strike. The pitcher wouldn't dare waste another. It would have to be somewhere around the plate. Yogi waited, shoulders hunched, head down, eyes steady on the pitcher.

Hudson leaned back and threw. Another curve, but this time Berra's bat connected and sent the ball skimming into right field for a clean single. Rizzuto scooted home and Yogi, grinning, stood safely on first. He had driven in his first run and made his first hit of 1949.

Casey started Berra the next day with Vic Raschi on the mound. The Yankees won, 3–0, but Yogi drew a blank at the plate. While the Bombers had won, Stengel was worried. Not only did the line-up lack DiMaggio and Keller, but Snuffy Stirnweiss was out and a couple of pitchers, Bob Porterfield and Clarence Marshall, were on the casualty list.

Yogi clouted his first homer of the season a few days later in Boston in a shocking 11–8 loss to the Red Sox. He was hit in the left hand while batting against the Senators in a night game at Washington, but took a more shattering jolt several days after that back at the Stadium when the Yankees were hosts to the Red Sox.

Lou Stringer, a pinch runner attempting to score from third on Johnny Pesky's short fly to Tommy Henrich in right field, crashed into Berra at the plate. Yogi was knocked for a loop, but managed to hold onto the ball and Stringer was out.

The Yankees surrounded the dazed catcher in an instant. "You all right?" a concerned Rizzuto asked. Yogi shook the cobwebs out of his head, looked up and nodded with a smile. His teammates helped him back to the dugout.

"That's stoppin' 'em," Dickey said, patting Yogi on the back.

While Stengel and Dickey were pleased with Berra's courage and his efforts as a receiver, they couldn't be happy with the results. One baseball writer described Berra as a "two-way blade which can cut the opposition or the Yankees impartially and unpredictably."

Yogi's average, hovering under the .250 mark, did not do justice to his value. He batted in runs, but he also allowed runs to score. Ed Lopat, canny southpaw veteran hurler, clearly showed his disgust with Berra when two wild heaves by the catcher set up four Boston runs which cost the Yankees the ball game.

This was the same Yogi who clubbed in five runs—one on a pinch homer—in the Red Sox series and without whom the Yankees would not have been leading the American League. Berra was a dilemma to Stengel as well as a delight.

Yogi got it from all sides in the month of May. Turning his head to glance at a disturbance in the stands during batting practice at Briggs Stadium before a game with the Detroit Tigers, Berra was struck in the head by a throw from Jackie Phillips.

Yogi fell to the ground like an empty sack and the players crowded around the unconscious catcher in worried clusters. He was carried off the field on a stretcher and rushed to the hospital, from whence came that famous medical

report which will linger in baseball history as long as there
is memory of Yogi Berra.

It went: "X rays of Berra's head showed nothing."

The laughs did not ease the pain of a badly bruised forehead and a discolored right eye for Yogi, whose near-
tragedy was turned to comedy.

The campaign brightened for Berra late in May, when
he socked his fourth homer and drove in four runs to help
blast the St. Louis Browns, 13–3. He finally lifted his batting average to .250 and led the club in the RBI department
with twenty-six.

Dickey was most exuberant about Yogi at this point.
"He's coming along, I tell you," he insisted to news hawks.
"You'll see. He's improved in every way."

In fact, Dickey opined, Berra would be the greatest
catcher in the game within two years. The writers scoffed.

"It all depends on him," Dickey said. "He has the natural ability and aptitudes except in one detail. He still
doesn't fall on the low ball that bounces in front of the
plate. Otherwise, Yogi is a sound receiver now."

Oddly, for all the talk about Berra's dumbness and
naïveté, Stengel respected Yogi's instinctive appraisal of a
pitcher's strength at any point in a ball game. The manager
always went along with his catcher's opinion.

Raschi was pitching one game and seemed to be weakening. A hit, a walk, another hit against big Vic and the
game halted while Casey slowly shuffled to the mound,
where he was joined by Berra and Rizzuto.

Casey put it up to Yogi. "What about him?" he asked,
motioning to Raschi.

"He's still got some stuff," Yogi whispered, "but he's
getting too cautious."

That was enough of a cue for Casey to lift Raschi and

signal to the bull pen for Tom Ferrick, who came in and saved Vic's triumph.

"I'd have let him stay in," Casey said later, "if Yogi told me to. The kid knows what this game's about."

By mid-June, Yogi's batting average was up to .280 and the Bronx Bombers were in first place, four games ahead of Detroit and six in front of Philadelphia. Berra greeted DiMaggio's return to the line-up on June 24th by walloping a double and a homer against the Tigers.

Yogi carried a .287 batting average into the All-Star game, for which he was named to share backstop chores with Birdie Tebbets of the Red Sox. The game was played at Ebbets Field in Brooklyn and, unfortunately, Berra did not perform illustriously in the American League's 11–7 victory over the National League. Yogi went hitless, but he caught well and no one stole on him.

The injury jinx which saddled the Yankees with seventy-two casualties for the 1949 season caught up with Berra in rough measure. At Cleveland, Larry Doby bowled him over attempting to steal home with the bases loaded and injured Yogi's elbow. Again, Berra made the out despite a stunning collision at the plate.

A few days later he pulled a muscle in his side, a recurrence of an old injury, which put him out of action again. Stengel was frantic. Henrich, casualty number forty-five for the season, was side-lined with a bruised toe. Charlie Silvera limped about with a twisted ankle, which left the Yanks with only Gus Niarhos behind the plate.

"We need Berra," Casey moaned. "We need his bat in that fifth spot in the batting order and we need him for the way he handles things behind the plate."

Yogi was back in action a few days later, beginning to substantiate Dickey's prediction that he would be the best catcher in the league. He was tremendous at bat. In a twin bill sweep of the St. Louis Browns on August 6th, Berra thundered out a grand slam home run that brought his RBI total to seventy-one, his homer output to fourteen and his batting average to .296.

The worst blow came the next day. The Yanks were pummeling the Browns, 20–2, when Dick Starr, a former Yankee hurler traded to St. Louis, caught Yogi on the hand with a fast ball. It caused a clean break of the thumb and Yogi, the Bombers' fiftieth casualty of the year, was out for at least three weeks.

Stengel raved, groaned, clutched his head, tore his hair. "Now . . . now with one of the toughest weeks of the season coming up," he despaired, "I lose one of my best men; in fact, one of the best I've ever seen since I came to the majors in 1912. Call it what you want, in my book it's tops in hard luck."

For Yogi, it was stark tragedy. He had begun to get the feel of his job and the confidence that comes with skill. There were twenty-nine steals, but only twelve could be attributed to him, and he had tossed out twenty-five would-be pilferers.

Besides, he was about to become a father. A little one was expected sometime that winter and Yogi, the breadwinner, wanted a solid reason for a salary raise.

"I've got to bear down," he told Rizzuto, his closest friend on the team. "Maybe a .300 average was all right before, but it isn't now. I was getting up to it . . . then this had to happen."

Phil never had seen Berra so low in spirits. "Don't worry, Yogi," he consoled. "You'll get back and get your share of the hits. Just make sure you're ready for the series."

"That's what worries me," Yogi muttered. "Getting into the series."

The Yankees managed to hang onto their lead while

Berra was absent. No one pestered the trainer or club physician Dr. Sidney Gaynor more than Berra, so anxious was he to return to harness.

He played for the first time on September 7th at Boston. The Yanks won, 5–2, but Berra went hitless in four times at bat. His thumb was still sore and swollen and jutted out like an extra finger. It was difficult for him to grip the bat properly.

His batting fell off as the Yankees' lead diminished. He was blanked as the Red Sox won, 3–0, and moved within a game of first place. Lopat lost a pitching duel to Ellis Kinder and Berra wore "the horns" with a bad throw to second which cost two runs.

The league race went into a frenzy two days later when the Red Sox beat the Yanks, 7–6, at the Stadium, but this time Yogi got in as a pinch hitter and drew a walk. The Bombers regained the lead and finally settled it with two wins at the Stadium in October, with Berra's bat booming again.

Brooklyn had won the National League flag so it was the Yankees against the Dodgers in the World Series, and a chance for Yogi to redeem himself against the club which had humiliated him two years before.

His thumb still pained excruciatingly and was twice its normal size. No amount of taping by Gus Mauch, the skillful Yankee trainer, could ease the agony when Berra swung.

"I only wish I could grip the bat," Yogi moaned, and Stengel moaned with him. Both knew how formidable the Dodgers could be in World Series play.

· 10 ·

Ebbets Field was jammed for the third game of the 1949 World Series.

The teams were even after two battles at the Stadium, a pair of 1–0 masterpieces by Allie Reynolds of the Yankees and Preacher Roe of the Dodgers. Now they were tied, 1–1, in the eighth inning in the smaller Brooklyn ball park with its short right field barrier and its frenzied rooters.

Yogi sensed the heightened tension of the crowd as he walked toward the plate with one out and lean-jawed Ralph Branca frowning at him from the mound. The fans weren't as noisy as they had been earlier. Their yips and screams now were muted to a low, growling roar.

"You back again?" It was Roy Campanella, the roly-poly Dodger catcher grimacing at him through his mask. Yogi shrugged and tapped the dirt off his cleats with the end of his bat. It hadn't been a good series for him.

Hitless in the first game, his thumb was still swollen and racked with pain. It was so bad that Stengel kept him out of the second game, but he had insisted on playing this one.

"It won't hurt if I can get wood on the ball," Yogi promised with beseeching eyes. Casey couldn't resist. If the kid wanted to play, he figured, let him play. Stengel

93

looked inquiringly at Gus Mauch, the trainer, who silently nodded assent.

Branca worked carefully on Berra even though he had gotten him out three times. The hurler remembered the pinch homer by the pudgy backstop in the 1947 series. He was determined not to give him anything good to hit this . time.

Yogi watched the first pitch break inside for ball one. The second was wide and very fast for ball two. He swung at the third, a sharp curve, but merely nicked it foul. The swing frightened Branca, who kept the next delivery wide.

Now Yogi waited for the fat one. Branca had to come in with it or walk him. The tall pitcher studied the stocky batter, the menacing looseness of his waggling bat at the plate, then wound up and threw. Ball four!

Yogi flipped his bat to the ground in disgust and trotted down the base line to first base. How he would have liked to bludgeon the ball into the stands!

Berra didn't dare steal on Campy, but he made a show of it off first base, prancing out and back. DiMaggio fouled out, but Bobby Brown rifled a single to right field and Yogi scooted around to third. Gene Woodling, always a dangerous batter, came up and Branca walked him to fill the bases.

The idea was to get at Cliff Mapes and hope for a double play, but shrewd Casey shuffled the deck. He sent up Johnny Mize to pinch-hit. The Big Cat, a lumbering giant with classic hitting form, had been passed up by Leo Durocher of Brooklyn in the deal which sent Mize from the Giants to the Yankees late in August.

Mize waited for the delivery, the heavy bat like a thin wand in his huge hands. Branca caught the corner with a fast one for a strike, then snapped over a fast curve for another. Dodger fans began to relax. In the Brooklyn dugout, Durocher stopped gnawing on his lip.

Branca tried another curve, low and inside. Mize's bat flashed and the ball streaked on a line to the wire screen in right field. Yogi pumped for all he was worth and tore into home for a precious run, turned to wait for Brown dashing in with another.

The Bombers led, 3–1, and Branca was finished. Jack Banta came in to face Gerry Coleman and was touched for a single which scored Woodling. It was the big marker, even though Luis Olmo and Campanella blasted homers in the ninth, making it 4–3, and Joe Page had to come in to fan Bruce Edwards in the last of the ninth.

"Nice work," Dickey said when Berra trudged in, his shin guards and chest protector still on. Yogi had called the pitches that struck out the Dodger pinch hitter and Page, the great Yankee relief twirler, had heeded him as a matter of course.

While Berra's receiving stood up nobly as the Yankees went on to capture the next two games and the World Series Championship, his batting was only slightly better than zero. Poor Yogi collected one hit in sixteen tries at the plate for a .063 series batting average.

"It's humiliating," he lamented to Carmen as they packed to leave their Bronx apartment near the Stadium. "Me," he added bitterly, "good field, no hit." It was baseball's classic description of the player who was brilliant with the glove and futile with the bat, the kind who fill the minor leagues.

Carmen smiled patiently at her husband. "Did you sign any autographs today," she asked.

"Yeah," Yogi drawled, puzzled. "What's that got to do with it?"

She cocked her head and directed a triumphant smile at him. "They followed you home?" she persisted.

"Yeah," Yogi answered, no restraint on his curiosity. "Okay, what's the pitch?"

She relented. "It's simple, dear. Kids don't follow catchers home; they follow hitters."

She bent over and kissed Yogi's cheek. He sat on the bed, comprehension dawning. "See?" she said, fussing over him affectionately before resuming her packing.

He perked up for a moment, then sagged glumly against the headboard. "What hitting? Don't you know my average for the season—.277?"

"Is that what you're going to tell Mr. Weiss when you start talking salary for next year?" she asked with a quizzical gleam.

Yogi smiled sheepishly. She had trapped him expertly.

"Don't be so hasty, Mrs. Berra," he laughed. "Don't forget those ninety-one runs batted in, those twenty homers. . . ."

They were a pleasant couple, simple in their tastes and mode of living, friendly but unobtrusive. When the Yankees were in town, they dined out or went to the movies in groups, mostly with the Phil Rizzutos, Frank Sheas and George Stirnweisses.

It was lonelier for Carmen when the team was on the road. She would visit with some of the other wives, go to shows, tend to her little chores in the apartment or read.

She had become a devoted baseball fan as the season progressed, learning much about the game sitting in a box seat with the other Yankee wives and from Yogi's comments at home.

In the first flush of domesticity, Carmen overdid the part one day at the Stadium. It was the fifth inning of a tight game with Cleveland when the young wife suddenly gasped.

"Please get Frank Scott for me immediately," she asked

an usher. "It's an emergency. I must get a message to Yogi."

Scott, traveling secretary for the Yankees at the time but now a highly successful business manager for close to one hundred baseball players, panted over, prepared for dire news.

"What is it, Carmen, what's wrong?" he gasped.

"Oh, Frank," she said, almost tearfully, "can you ask Yogi whether he wants pork chops or lamb chops for dinner tonight? I forgot to ask. . . ." Her voice trailed off weakly at the look of amazement and relief on Scott's face.

Lawrence Allen Berra, eight pounds five ounces, was born December 8th. The Berras were living in Yogi's old home on Elizabeth Street in St. Louis with his parents and kid sister. Josie. The three other Berra boys were married and in their own homes.

Yogi had remodeled the eight-room house, even to installing a wood-paneled rumpus room in the basement. He was happy at home in the winter, visiting old haunts with his pals, seeing his family, bowling, golfing and even playing soccer.

He was the same old Yogi—uncomplicated, good natured and unpretentious. Although he did play golf occasionally with Stan Musial at the Sunset Country Club and ran off with some baseball buddies for a few days at Hot Springs, Arkansas, he also spent a great deal of time with his pals on The Hill.

Yogi was no clothes horse. Hatless, wrapped in a favorite leather jacket, hands dug into his pockets, he walked across The Hill, head down, like any fellow on the neighborhood. No one could mistake him for a celebrity.

His daily routine was settled but comfortable that winter. He stayed up late at night, and arose late in the morning. He ate a big breakfast, read all the available newspapers and then took a brisk walk. Although he owned a flashy late model car, Yogi preferred to use his sturdy legs.

His brother John, a waiter at Henry Ruggeri's restaurant on Edwards Street, talked Yogi into becoming a greeter there. Donned in a tuxedo, his hair slicked back and a professional smile on his face, Yogi welcomed patrons during the dinner hours.

The proud proprietor, a baseball fan and a friend of the Berras from way back, even had cards printed which read: "YOUR GENIAL HOST LAWRENCE (YOGI) BERRA, WORLD'S CHAMPION YANKEE CATCHER, GREETS YOU FROM RUGGERI'S."

Ruggeri's was a fine establishment, urbane and fairly expensive. Yogi often felt out of place there himself, even when he glanced in the mirror at his tuxedoed figure. He felt a tug of sympathy for a young couple, obviously on a first date, who seemed nervous and uncomfortable in the plush setting.

Yogi put them at their ease immediately. "It's just like a hamburger joint," he assured them, "only with table-cloths and a bigger menu."

But even his own wonderful home town, with its familiar flavor and friendships, palled on Yogi after a while. Thoughts of baseball, the crack of bat meeting ball, the crunching sound of cleats digging into the base paths, the odors of liniment in the clubhouse, the thud of a pitch whomping into the mitt created a strange yearning within him.

Carmen read the signs. "You can't wait," she said. "You're anxious to play ball again, aren't you?"

Yogi managed a wan smile. "I have a feeling this'll be a big season for me," he said earnestly. "I'm due . . . I know it."

But eager as he was to play ball, he didn't intend to rush into a new contract. George Weiss, the Yankee general manager, discovered that quickly when a contract for sixteen thousand, five hundred dollars, a substantial raise over Berra's 1949 figure, was returned unopened.

Carmen was amazed when Yogi picked up the bulky letter which contained the Yankee contract and sent it back without reading the terms.

"Yogi," she exclaimed, "you don't know how much they're offering!"

He grimaced. "Honey, whatever it is, isn't enough." And pointing to the letter, he added: "Not in this one."

When the Yankees assembled in St. Petersburg without Berra, still unsigned, Stengel began to haunt Weiss. The Yankee manager couldn't rest until he saw his squat slugger safely in camp and working into condition.

Finally, Weiss invited Yogi down to St. Petersburg at club expense. A wily gentleman, Weiss knew full well the softening effects of the balmy baseball weather on a restive character like Berra. The plan worked—partially.

Yogi wanted twenty-two thousand dollars and wouldn't budge. Casey became frantic. The fear that the financial sit-down would bring Berra into camp too far out of shape and possibly kill off all Yankee chance of a fast getaway in the American League race gave Casey nightmares.

When Berra finally capitulated, it was for eighteen thousand dollars. After the signing, Yogi admitted to Rizzuto that he couldn't resist the urge to play. "The next time I hold out," he promised, "I'll stay up north in the ice and snow. Who can keep away from the diamond down here?"

Casey's greeting on Yogi's entrance to the St. Pete clubhouse was effusive.

"Glad to see you, Larry," Stengel said, with a low bow. "You're my catcher, kid, the one which works the close games." Casey had an oratorical style all his own, logic spiced with wit and jumbled double talk, except that when listened to carefully, it made sense.

"Yes, sir," he continued, apparently addressing the entire clubhouse group, "there's the man which caught two World Series in three years. They laughed at him, but they're not laughing any more." This was followed by another huge wink at the red-faced Berra.

"They said he'd murder us, but he murdered them. He looks funny. He wears his shin guards wrong, but he does a job for you."

Yogi, inching his embarrassed way toward the door, slipped out of the room during the next tirade.

"He doesn't look graceful," Casey rambled on, "and he's not perfect with those throws, but you don't have to take him out of there. He knows what to do. And he can hit that apple."

Someone pointed out that Yogi had departed and the build-up job could stop.

"Build-up job?" the Yankee boss screamed, turning to Dickey. "How about it, Bill? Can he block those low balls? Can he protect the plate?"

Dickey had to laugh. "I'll say this," he conceded, "I never got out after a bunt as fast as this kid does and I couldn't get a pop fly faster, either."

All the Yankees were happy to see Yogi around, not only for what his bat could do to make them richer citizens come October, but for the life and jollity he added to the general atmosphere.

No one appreciated more than Berra what a good season, free from injury, could mean to his career. "Just for once," he told Rizzuto, "I'd like to go through the schedule without putting Dr. Gaynor to work."

One of the players kidded him about his tendency to

swing at bad pitches. "Joe Medwick's still my hero," Yogi insisted stoutly. Medwick, the old St. Louis Cardinal slugger, was considered the greatest bad-ball hitter in baseball.

"Yeah, I'd like to be able to wait for those good pitches like Ted Williams does," Berra said. "But everyone has his style. I swing off my ear and I get hits."

"Don't worry, Yogi," Bobby Brown chimed in. "As long as the pitchers are scared, it means you're doing all right."

It was a successful and peaceful training season for Berra. By the end of March he was battering the ball consistently and performing his receiving chores with mechanical efficiency beyond anything he had ever displayed before.

Before an exhibition game with the Cardinals, Joe Garagiola walked over to watch the Yankee batters take their cuts. "You know what made him a good catcher?" he said, motioning toward his boyhood pal.

"Catching every day," he went on, answering his own question. "I'm not telling the manager what he ought to do, but catching every day makes a good catcher." Joe's career had not progressed as well as he had hoped. The fans, although not as brutal as in 1948, still gave him a rough time in St. Louis.

He watched Berra lunge at the ball. "He's no dummy. A lot of guys making fun of him would like to earn his money."

Stengel ambled over. "He'd hit .350 if he learned to let the first pitch go by. Too anxious to hit. The pitchers take advantage. He's gotta let some of 'em go by."

He paused to watch Yogi bang a few shots deep to the outfield with his eccentric batting style.

"Hard to figure," Stengel said, shaking his wise old head. "But he gets results and you don't want to spoil that."

"What's Yogi got?" an onlooker asked.

"Most hitters uppercut the ball," Casey analyzed. "But this guy swings downward. That's why the ball travels so far and straight."

He sighed. "He could hit .350 . . . if he laid off the first pitch."

· 11 ·

St. Louis is a sweltering city in midsummer, unbearably hot and uncomfortable for ballplayers.

But it was home to Yogi, and sitting in shorts near an open window of the visitors' dressing room in Sportsman's Park, the Yankee catcher didn't mind the heat.

Red Patterson, the Yankee publicity director, riffled through the records books spread out on a table before him. "I'll find it," he insisted, "I'll find it."

"Uh, uh," Yogi said, shaking his head in the negative. "Your figures are wrong. I've been up 332 times, not 335. And I've batted in 67 runs, not 66. I count 'em myself."

Phil Rizzuto looked up from a newspaper. "Yogi doesn't trust anyone with his hitting figures," he said, then stuck his head back into the sports section.

"I'll tell you another thing," Yogi resumed. "I bet you don't know it, but I'm on another hitting streak."

"Seven games, isn't it?" Patterson said.

"Eight," Yogi corrected. "I got a single pinch-hitting against the White Sox last week and I've hit in all seven games since I came back."

Patterson banged his books shut and swept them to the side with mock disgust. "Whaddya know," he railed. "The guy's right. Maybe we oughta trade jobs."

Yogi grinned wickedly. He wasn't through with Red yet.

"I had two ten-game hitting streaks this year and you got me down for only one," he said. "Check that and you'll see I'm right."

Patterson nosed through his books again. "All right," he conceded, "you got me dead. I'm handing in my resignation when we get home."

"Fat chance," someone muttered. It was July 24, 1950, and the beginning of a Yankee swing through the West. The Bombers trailed the Detroit Tigers for first place by one game.

They had dropped a tough one to the Tigers in New York in their last game before this western trip. Berra had socked a homer that put his team ahead, but the Bengals rallied and won the game.

Yogi's bat had come to life in vibrant fashion since the Yankees traveled through this area earlier in the season. He hit .228 on that trip through the badlands, possibly even worse than the average implied because he got most of his whacks against the Browns.

He spent a nightmarish time in Chicago, Detroit and Cleveland, with only seven safeties in thirty eight times at bat for a .172 mark, including six hitless games.

Then Yogi found his eye and began to pummel the ball. His batting average rose to .319 and his presence at the plate meant worrisome moments for opposition pitchers.

His catching had matched progress with his hitting. Yogi made a couple of throws in the Detroit series which were nothing short of sensational. He cut down runners several times after they had gotten such big jumps he didn't seem to have a chance of nipping them.

Back of the plate, Berra worked with a quiet confidence that marked his development as a receiver. He handled the pitchers flawlessly and, best of all, now stopped the low pitches which are a catcher's most difficult job.

Exactly how much Yogi meant to the Yankee pitching staff became a favorite debate between Stengel and the press. The more Casey insisted Berra was the guiding hand behind the mound corps, the more the writers scoffed and put it down to Stengel soft-soaping. Soft-soaping, that is, of Berra. They felt the canny manager was using them in his campaign to make the gullible Berra believe he was a reincarnation of Roger Bresnahan, Mickey Cochrane and Bill Dickey wrapped into one.

The baseball writers' amused resistance to his appraisal of Berra annoyed Stengel at first, but it turned to smug vindication as the season progressed and Berra's all-round improved play became so apparent no one could dispute it.

"He's the boss out there," Stengel told the writers in his cramped office underneath the Stadium grandstand. "Yogi knows what he's doing all the time. He says a man's still got it, I go with him," Casey said earnestly. "He says the pitcher is weakening, I signal the bull pen and get someone heating up." Casey look around defiantly at the reporters, daring anyone to challenge his views. No one did. If they laughed at all now, it was with Yogi, not at him.

Not only had Berra cut down on the base stealers, he himself was getting on the bags more often. He stopped swinging at so many bad pitches. He still reached out for and golfed some of his hits, but his concept of the strike zone area had narrowed.

The alertness and innate baseball knowledge which wiser baseball heads had spotted in his rookie years emerged to more noticeable proportions in Yogi now. He became one of the Yankees' best base runners.

"The kid's begging me for the steal sign all the time," Stengel chattered. "He's got the pitchers' motions down so pat he takes terrific leads off the bag." Casey winked. "Maybe he's paying some of these guys back for what they did to him on the bases."

As a hitter, Berra no longer found southpaw hurlers irksome. Against left sidearm pitching, he used to fall away from the plate so far he ended up practically with his back to the mound. Even Joe McCarthy, the old Yankee boss who shifted over to managership of the Red Sox, discovered the futility of trying to stymie Yogi with portside chucking.

Berra opened a nine-run Yankee inning against the Bosox with a single off Mel Parnell, a left-hander, and when he came up again in the same frame, McCarthy brought in Earl Johnson, a southpaw side-wheeler.

The Boston bench, taking the cue from McCarthy, got on Yogi immediately. "Let's see you turn around, Ugly Man," they shouted. "Fall back, fall back, don't get that pretty face ruined."

Johnson wound up deliberately, bent far over and came around with a low, sweeping motion. Berra stepped into it with a sharp swing and clouted the ball through the infield for another clean hit and another run driven in.

Yogi's bat, his catching and his personality had been a tonic for the Yankees all through the arduous 1950 campaign. The consistency of his stickwork, his frequent streaks at the plate and his enormously helpful clutch hitting actually kept the Bombers going.

In July, scrambling to overhaul the league-leading Tigers while holding off the Cleveland Indians and Boston Red Sox, the New Yorkers moved into a vital series with the Philadelphia Athletics in the Stadium. The Yankees won the game, 12–8, chiefly because Yogi got on base three times, twice on walks and once on a single.

The nation's baseball fans appreciated Yogi as much as his teammates did. They voted him number one catcher ahead of Birdie Tebbets of the Red Sox for the American League team in the All-Star game in Chicago.

The National Leaguers won, 4–3, and Yogi went hitless in two at-bats, the second straight year he had failed to connect in All-Star competition.

There were extenuating circumstances once again. In 1949 it had been a badly swollen thumb. This year it was a painfully injured knee which he had hurt diving after a foul pop in Boston almost two weeks before the All-Star affair.

He had played for ten days with the bad knee and refused to pull out of the All-Star assignment. "I got into the game in the fifth inning last year," he told Rizzuto en route to Chicago, "but this is the first time the fans voted me in as a starter and I'll be there if I have to play on crutches."

The Yankees had just defeated the Red Sox, 3–1, behind Ed Lopat, and Berra had drive in the first of two runs in the first inning with a slashing single, adding a double later in the game. He could run straight without trouble, but any pressure left or right was agonizing and it hurt to squat in the backstop position.

By the end of July, his knee having healed, Yogi went on a hitting rampage that lifted the Yankees to the top. He belted his eleventh homer of the season in the first game of a double-header sweep in Detroit and his twelfth in the nightcap along with a pair of doubles.

Vic Raschi started the opener but weakened to the extent of serving up two home run balls and Berra gave Stengel the sign for another pitcher. Joe Ostrowski came in and finished the job. Tom Ferrick had to save the second game for the faltering Fred Sanford with a double-play ball to the Tigers' Marv Rickert.

The Yankees were in trouble in what amounted to a four-team struggle for the pennant. Stengel summed it up best on August 30th, when the Bombers went ahead of the Tigers by one game.

The Yankees were about to open a series with the Indians. "We don't hit enough," Casey told Joe Williams, Scripps-Howard columnist. "We got to scramble for runs even against the weak clubs. After the pitchers get past Berra and DiMaggio, they can stop bleeding."

At that point the Yankees had seen thirty-three of their games decided by one run, nineteen in their favor and fourteen for the opposition. It supported Stengel's contention that his club needed more batting punch.

Casey credited the presence of Whitey Ford, a rookie promoted from the Kansas City farm team on June 29th, with saving the mound staff. "We'd have been dead without him," Stengel admitted, as well he might in view of the nine straight victories the little left-hander contributed that season.

Berra was keeping his batting average up, but the Bombers weren't staying with him. The Tigers went ahead again September 8th by beating Chicago, 3–2, while the Yankees were idle, and the Bengals stayed there until the crucial series with the Yankees in Detroit which began September 14th.

DiMaggio, Mize and Cliff Mapes blasted homers and Raschi twirled a seven-hitter for his twentieth win as the Yanks climbed over the Tigers in the opener. The next day, Detroit was on top again with a 9–7 win in a wild-swinging affray, despite three homers by Big Jawn Mize.

It was the sixth time in his long career that Mize had hit three home runs in one game. Only once, however, did his prodigious clouting result in a victory. "I'm going to have to stop hitting three homers a game," he lamented.

The game that broke the Tigers back took place on September 16th before fifty-six thousand at Briggs Stadium. Ford and Dizzy Trout hooked up in a nerve-racking mound duel for eight innings, with the Bombers leading, 1–0, on DiMaggio's homer in the sixth.

The roof fell in on the Bengals in the ninth, when Yankee bats hammered out seven runs and salted the game away at 8–1. New York never relinquished the league lead again and finally wound up three full games ahead of the Tigers.

The 1950 World Series against the Philadelphia Phillies was anticlimactic after the Yankees' furious fight to win the American League pennant.

Anti-climactic for the Yankees, perhaps, but desperately disappointing for the Phillies, who had beaten out the Brooklyn Dodgers for the National League flag on the final day of the season in a ten-inning thriller ended by Dick Sisler's home run.

Casey Stengel's Bombers swept the baseball classic in four straight games, not by bombing feats but on superb pitching against a weary but gallant foe.

Eddie Sawyer, manager of the Whiz Kids, faced severe problems, foremost of which was a twirling ace suffering from "combat fatigue." Robin Roberts, ace right-hander, had pitched three games in the final five days of the National League race.

Sawyer, in a surprise move, called on Jim Konstanty, bespectacled relief expert who had appeared in seventy-four games, a major league record, for the opener against Vic Raschi of the Yankees.

Big Vic threw a two-hitter, walked only one Philly and struck out five, with Berra calling a perfect game behind the plate. "I never shook him off once," an elated Raschi said after the 1–0 triumph.

Bobby Brown's double and a pair of outfield fly balls by

Hank Bauer and Gerry Coleman in the fourth inning scored the winning run. The Yankees collected only five hits, none by Berra.

Yogi connected for an unproductive single in the second game, but DiMaggio's homer with Coleman on in the tenth inning was the pay-off clout in the 2–1 win over Roberts. Allie Reynolds limited the Phillies to seven hits.

The Yankees won the third game back home in the Stadium, 3–2, for Ed Lopat in which Coleman again came through with the timely hit. The perky second baseman's single scored Gene Woodling in the ninth to break a tie.

The fourth and final series contest, 5–2 in the Yankees favor, saw Berra finally come to life as a batter in the fall classic. Yogi walloped a single and a homer in four at-bats, driving in two runs for Whitey Ford's victory.

Reynolds had to sew it up with two out in the ninth, after two runs crossed the plate on Willie Jones's single, a hit batsman and Woodling's error on Andy Seminick's fly. Mike Goliat singled and Stengel didn't even have to query Berra. He motioned to Reynolds who finished it off by fanning Stan Lopata.

Yogi was jubilant in the clubhouse. "I got the bat working at last," he glowed.

During the Yankee victory celebration that night, Rizzuto drew Berra aside. "You're gonna be a big man now," the Scooter said. "You can make a lot of money if you stay east. How about it?"

Yogi's brow wrinkled. He had given the move thought since the summer, but his mother fell and broke her hip and was still in a wheel chair. Besides, Carmen's mother was seriously ill in Salem, Missouri.

"I'll have to think it over, Phil," he said sadly. Rizzuto sighed. He had a number of good business deals lined up for Yogi, to whom he had grown very close as roommate and counsellor.

Berra returned to the celebration with not a worry in the world.

Hadn't he batted .322 for the season, walloped twenty-seven homers, driven in one hundred twenty-four runs and played in one hundred fifty-one games?

· 12 ·

Yogi, Carmen and their husky baby son spent the winter on Elizabeth Street on The Hill, but they weren't as happy as in the past.

Yogi found it almost impossible to be himself, even with old pals. He was too well known, too popular and too sought after by a public which overlooked Yogi Berra, the man, and saw only Yogi Berra, the Yankee catcher.

Besides, as Rizzuto had forewarned, his fame carried obligations: invitations to speak at banquets, lodge meetings, business gatherings, Boy Scout meetings, school functions—all these took time and energy. There were endorsements and television appearances, too.

The personal appearance demands on Yogi became unbearable. At home in St. Louis he had no one but Carmen and himself to handle negotiations. It led to unpleasant experiences with sometimes thoughtless and unpleasant people who had no regard for a baseball player's private life.

The phone rang one night and Yogi answered. It was the chairman of the entertainment committee for a lodge banquet. The man not only was insistent but peremptory in his demands that Yogi speak at an affair over one hundred miles away from St. Louis.

The chairman didn't ask Berra to appear; he demanded it as though Yogi were in bondage.

It grated on the extraordinarily amenable Yogi to the point where finally he interjected: "How about expenses?"

There was a shocked silence for a while.

"Don't the Yankees pay you?" came the condescending reply. "If you can't manage it, maybe we can scrape up something for your gas."

Yogi hung up but it was hours before his composure returned. It wasn't the money. He never asked to be paid for appearing at these functions.

"Back east," he told Carmen, "the Yankee office would handle all of this. We wouldn't be bothered." It was a telling point.

They managed to spend a great deal of time in New York, however, because of several TV appearances. Carmen loved the theaters and night life of New York. Yogi reveled in the big-time sports available there, particularly basketball and hockey.

Before Yogi left for camp in Phoenix, Arizona—the Yankees had traded spring training bases with the New York Giants for the 1951 season—the Berras decided to move East and selected a site in suburban Woodcliff Park, New Jersey.

The Yankees found it far more difficult, however, to sign him up for the 1951 season. There was a slight difference of opinion, amounting to fifteen thousand dollars, between Yogi and General Manager George Weiss.

Yogi was asking forty thousand dollars to sign his contract for 1951. Weiss was offering twenty-five thousand. Berra wouldn't budge and neither would Weiss.

From the Yankee office came a proclamation that Berra was asking double what any other catcher was earning in the majors, that at the rate he was getting raises he would be drawing two hundred thousand dollars before long and that he was too young for such big money.

The Yankees were in camp a week and still Yogi sat it out in St. Louis. "I've already sent back two contracts," he said, "and I'll keep on sending 'em back until I get what I deserve. It isn't as if I'm just being stubborn," he added. "I came down a bit but they won't come up a buck."

The newspapers were full of the Battle of the Buck, as they called it, but anyone who understood baseball realized the Yankees needed Berra. Stengel was the first to go to bat for him with Weiss. Knowing how much he needed the work, he couldn't stand to look out at his athletes cavorting on the diamond without seeing Berra in a monkey suit, too.

Resistance on both sides collapsed on February 28th when Yogi and the Yankees settled on a figure of thirty thousand dollars. Berra headed for camp the same night and pulled into the Yankee hotel in Phoenix at two o'clock the next morning.

"I'm in shape," he reported with a grin. "Had my own basketball team and we wore shirts with Yogi printed on 'em."

He wasn't kidding about being in condition and proved it quickly enough outdoors. Not only that, he was as eager and exuberant as a rookie.

"What would you say if I told you I might shoot for the American League batting championship in another year?" he asked Dan Daniel, sports writer for the New York World-Telegram and Sun.

He wasn't getting a swelled head, Yogi explained, just smarter up at the plate. He was taking Stengel's teachings to heart about swinging for pitches up around his ears and down around his ankles.

"Last season I drew fifty-five walks," Yogi said. "The year before that I got only twenty-two. Suppose it had been that few last year. My .322 batting average would have been only .305."

Only one thing bothered Yogi: a newspaper story head-lined, "Ruth Had His Gehrig, DiMaggio's Got His Berra."

"Is this a boost or a knock?" he puzzled. It was a story that compared the great Babe Ruth–Lou Gehrig slugging combination of the Yankees' Murderers Row days to the DiMaggio–Berra duo.

Frank Shea, Joe Collins and some of the other Bombers assured him that it was an entirely complimentary story.

"Sometimes," Yogi conceded, "it's tough to tell what these guys write about." He was sensitive about stories which appeared to make him seem foolish or stupid, par-ticularly since they also irritated Carmen.

Although Berra reported a week late, it didn't take him long to attain peak physical condition. He concluded spring training with a .397 average, including three homers among his twenty-seven hits. It was taken for granted by everyone that he would be a big gun in 1951.

Nevertheless, when the regulation American League campaign started, Yogi found himself in what amounted to a slump. He collected a meager four hits in his first nine-teen times at bat during the opening week for a dismal .238 average.

"My timing is off," he grumbled to Stengel. "I can't get my body into the sock."

"You're swinging late," Casey told him. "You and the rest of 'em."

None of the Yankee sluggers was hitting. DiMaggio was at .273, Mize at .196 and Rizzuto, voted the Most Valuable Player the previous season, was hitting .211.

"I'm calling a special batting drill tomorrow morning," the manager told his aides. "Either that or turn some of these birds into pitchers."

The long workout helped Berra, who lashed a single and drew two walks as the Bombers beat the A's, 5–4, behind Raschi's six-hit hurling. Yogi wasn't too pleased about the passes, but he took solace from the solid feel of his lone hit.

"It ain't much use getting your timing right," he told Bobby Brown, "if you're gonna keep the bat on your shoulder."

Brown gave him a sly look. "You're getting on base, aren't you?" he queried.

"Nuts," Yogi grimaced. "If a guy's gonna lead the league in hitting or in homers, he's gotta swing. That's what I aim to be doing from now on."

"What's the big rush, boy?" drawled Mize, who had ambled over. "Give some of us older guys a chance to make it first."

"Can't afford it, Jawn," Yogi said. "We got a new member of the family arriving in September . . . you know, another mouth to feed. I need that World Series dough."

By early June, Berra knew he was earning the raise he had held out for during the winter. He was the work horse of the team, perhaps of the entire league. He caught forty-one of the Yankees' first forty-four games, and was out only when he bruised his arm in Chicago, May 1st, when he was rested for two days.

But the long hours were taking something out of the stumpy little catcher. There seemed to be more extra-inning games for the Bombers than ever before, more three-and-two situations, more wild pitches and more walks.

The Yankees didn't give Berra many easy games to catch. Tommy Byrne was never wilder on the mound. Fred Sanford, Raschi and even Reynolds wasted too many pitches. All this, coupled with the necessity of keeping a rein on the runners allowed on with base hits and walks, gave Yogi a trying time.

But where others bogged down or weakened, Berra stayed in there playing his game. He walloped his eighth homer on June 5th to help beat the Indians for the Yankees' first triumph in four games. His backstopping was superb, for Reynolds had the ball sailing all afternoon. Allie walked six men, five to lead-off batters, which meant extra vigilance for Yogi.

A month later, on July 6th, his batting average was .309 and rising as he went on a ten-game hitting streak that lifted the club to five wins in their last eight games. He unloaded a homer and double to beat Bobby Shantz of the Athletics, the second blow a clutch rap with two out in the ninth.

"I'm not swinging for the seats any more," Yogi confided to Rizzuto after that game. He had been trying too hard, pressing for the big one on the last western trip and had fallen into a slump. "I'm just hitting with the pitch."

"Who stuck that idea in your head?" Phil asked in amazement. He knew how Berra liked to bruise the ball.

"I heard Casey talking to that kid," Yogi said with a shy grin, looking over toward a powerfully built blond youngster with enormous shoulders and a huge neck. It was Mickey Mantle, a rookie with a fantastic reputation as a belter.

Phil was intrigued. "What'd he say?" the shortstop asked.

Yogi waved his hands aimlessly. "Oh, Case told him he didn't have to kill the ball to drive it into the stands. Just hit easy and let his natural power do the work."

Phil didn't say a word, just eyed him quizzically.

"So I figured I'm a pretty strong guy and it should work for me," Yogi finished self-consciously.

"Well, whaddya know," murmured Phil, laughing. "An eavesdropper. . . ." He was stopped by a damp towel square in the face.

"Yeah," he heard Yogi growl. "With your average, maybe you oughta drop a couple of eaves once in a while."

The Yankees were in third place, one game behind the Chicago White Sox and another behind the Boston Red Sox, at the All-Star game recess on July 10th in Detroit. And for the fourth time Berra was on the American League roster.

The National Leaguers won, 8–3, but Yogi caught the entire game in impressive fashion and contributed a hit that led to the American Leaguers' first run. "That game should do me a lot of good," he chirped cheerfully. "My timing seems a lot better."

Stengel once again was desperate for power. DiMaggio suffered a pull in his left leg in Boston and had to cancel out of the All-Star game. Jolting Joe, in a terrible slump, needed the rest and informed Stengel he would be out for at least ten days.

The Yankees were involved in a hectic, unpredictable race in the junior loop. The White Sox had scrambled to the top in May, only to be supplanted by the Boston Red Sox in July. Now it was the Yankees and the Cleveland Indians tugging and hauling at each other for the lead.

Reynolds pitched his first of two no-hitters for the 1951 season on July 12th at Cleveland, besting Bob Feller, 1–0, in a thrilling duel broken up by Gene Woodling's seventh-inning homer.

One of the four hits Feller yielded was a bunt single by Berra in the ninth which went for naught. The last of the ninth was a spine tingler. Reynolds fanned pinch hitter Bob Lemon and got Dale Mitchell on a feeble grounder to Coleman.

Bobby Avila, a keen-eyed hitter, came up. The tension was high in the stands and on the field. Allie, big and calm, waited for Yogi's signal. Working carefully, he brought the count to two balls and one strike.

Yogi squatted, signaled for the curve and waited for the delivery. Even the loquacious Berra was grimly silent now. Reynolds' arm flashed back and then he threw, putting so much on the curve that he fell forward on his face. It was wide and Yogi barely gathered it in.

Allie blazed the next one inside and across the knees for a three-two count. Avila dug in, eyes squinting into the glare.

"All right, Allie boy," Yogi coaxed. "Let's get this one . . . let's get it. . . ."

The ball shot in, waist high, and Avila swung. The ball dipped elusively and plunked into Yogi's mitt. Strike three! It was over! A no-hitter for Reynolds.

Gratifying as this feat was, it couldn't get the Yankees up into the lead. Cleveland built up a three-game cushion in first place by August 23rd before suddenly falling into a slump which dropped them back in September.

The turning point came on September 16th and 17th against the Indians in the Stadium as the Bombers beat Bob Feller, 5–1, and Bob Lemon, 2–1, to initiate a streak which won them nine of their next twelve games and put them in front to stay.

Reynolds administered the *coup de grâce* to the Boston Red Sox in the Stadium on September 28th with his second no-hitter of the season, a classic which almost slipped out of Berra's mitt with two out in the ninth.

It was the first game of a twin bill, the Bombers leading, 8–0, with two out and Ted Williams at bat. Wasting no time and no pitches, Allie burned two fast strikes over. The next pitch was a streak of white, but Williams, whipping the bat around with the great wrist action which is his hallmark, caught a piece of the ball.

Up and up it went, a high, twisting foul back of the plate. Yogi was after it instantly, racing to where he judged it would land as he kept his gaze aloft.

The ball began its descent, the spin imparting unusual force. Yogi made a grab for it as it shot down suddenly to the left. Squirming as if alive, the ball struck the pocket of his mitt as he sprawled forward, then it twisted out and fell to the ground.

The crowd groaned. Yogi got up with a sick feeling. He hated to face Reynolds, whose no-hitter hung on a slender thread. To give a batsman of Williams' caliber a second chance was tempting fate too much.

Yogi shuffled out to the mound, his face a tragic mask. "I'm sorry, Allie," he began falteringly. . . .

"Forget it," the pitcher said. Reynolds seemed amazingly cheerful and confident. "Don't worry, Yogi," he grinned, patting Berra's back, "we'll get him again."

Berra called for the low hard one and again Ted sent a skyrocket foul up behind the plate—another twister, even tougher than the last shot.

Yogi dashed out, determined not to let it get away. His last-minute lunge trapped the rapidly spinning ball securely. It was over, a reprieve for him and a second no-hitter for Allie.

The American League race was as good as finished from that point. The Yankees shot ahead to a five-game final margin over the Indians and eleven in front of the third-place Boston Red Sox.

Now they waited while Leo Durocher's Giants, making a storybook finish with a great stretch drive from thirteen and a half games behind to overhaul the Brooklyn Dodgers on the last day of the season, won a special three-game play-off for the National League pennant.

The Giants took the first play-off game, 3–1, and the

Dodgers ran away with the second, 10–0. Then, trailing by two runs in the ninth with one out and two men on base, the Giants' Bobby Thomson smashed his historic homer off Ralph Branca to clinch the game and the flag.

The Giants continued their Cinderella career in the World Series. Durocher's surprise mound choice in the opener was Dave Koslo, a chunky veteran southpaw, who beat Reynolds, 5–1, as Monte Irvin got four hits and stole home and Alvin Dark poled a three-run homer.

It looked like a rout, but Ed Lopat's solid five-hitter halted the Polo Grounders, 3–1, in the second contest. The Giants went ahead again, winning the third, 6–2, when Eddie Stanky, apparently caught stealing second, kicked the ball out of Phil Rizzuto's glove, and Berra dropped a throw on a sure out at the plate a bit later.

Then came a providential two-day rain, which seemed to cool the red-hot Giants and to give Reynolds the additional rest he needed to come back strong as a bull. And after three hitless games, DiMaggio exploded a homer and single to wrap it up, 6–2.

The fifth game was a walkover—13–1—behind Lopat's five-hitter, with rookie Gil McDougald whacking a grand slam homer. The final game, at the Stadium, was tight until Hank Bauer tripled off Koslo with the bases loaded to assure a 4–3 victory.

Yogi may have been a weary young man after the series, but it didn't stop him from celebrating.

"This is the tops," he kept telling anyone who would listen in the pandemonium of the Yankee clubhouse after the series clincher.

It never occurred to the modest and hard-working Yogi that greater honors lay ahead, that the batting average which had dwindled to .294 at the season's end was not the only measure of his value.

· 13 ·

The phone rang and Yogi stretched his hand out lazily for it. He was propped up comfortably on a huge settee in the spacious, yet cozy, living room of his home in quiet, suburban Woodcliff Park, New Jersey.

Who can that be, he wondered, for a moment debating whether or not to answer. He had spent a busy morning and afternoon teaching ambitious youngsters the fine points of baseball at Phil Rizzuto's winter school in a New York City armory.

In the evening, he put in a long stint as a celebrity salesman in a large Newark clothing store, another job that came to him through Rizzuto. It was surprising how many people were willing to be fitted for a suit of clothes by a man whose only training for the task was donning his own baseball uniform.

The work wasn't arduous, but it left Yogi drained of desire to talk. Amiable and gregarious though he was, he had his limits, too. The constant greeting and small chitchat with fans and their youngsters took an enormous toll in nervous energy.

The phone rang insistently. From the kitchen, where she was preparing a snack for him, Yogi heard Carmen answer on the extension. "It's for you, dear," she called out. He picked up the receiver.

It was the Associated Press. "Yogi," the voice vibrated across the wires from New York, "they've just named you MVP for 1951!"

Yogi moved the receiver away from his ear and gazed at it in astonishment. Yogi Berra the Most Valuable Player in the American League? It was fantastic. A joke, maybe.

There was dead silence for a few moments and then he could hear the scratching query on the other end of the line. "Yogi . . . hey, are you on . . . ?"

Carmen stood in the doorway, concern in her lovely dark eyes.

"It's some guy says I won the MVP," Yogi explained with a shrug. He returned to the phone.

The news was true. Now he recognized the voice of the A.P. reporter, a person who wouldn't joke about something this important.

The phone didn't stop ringing that night. In an hour the house was crowded with reporters, photographers, newsreel cameramen and a television crew.

"I still think they shoulda picked Reynolds," Berra kept repeating to his friends among the baseball writers. "Honest, I never thought I'd get it. I figured to be in the voting, sure, but Wahoo pitched seven shut-outs, a couple of no-hitters and he was our hot man with those seventeen wins."

Rizzuto, who rushed over when he got the news, poked Berra. "What's the matter," he exploded, "don't you want it?"

"Oh, I'm not giving it away," Yogi laughed nervously. "Just that I didn't figure it . . . you know, my batting slump the last two weeks and all. . . ."

The excitement was at last beginning to reach him. His hands trembled and he spoke with a distracted air. Carmen took him into the kitchen and closed the door. She put her arms around him and kissed him gently.

"Honey," she said softly, "relax. You deserved it. It's not so startling." She went on in that vein, soothing and cajoling until Yogi gradually relaxed.

"I'm all right now, baby," he said after a while. "I better get out there." They were shouting for him, their cameras and sound equipment all set up and ready for the interview. "Don't worry," the new MVP said, winking at her as he strode into the living room.

The next day was more frenzied. Berra was swamped with congratulators wherever he went. At the armory in mid-Manhattan, the pupils in the baseball school besieged him. "We'll never get any work done here today," Rizzuto piped with mock anger.

The MVP voting had selected pitcher Ned Garver, a twenty-game winner for the hapless St. Louis Browns, second and Reynolds third. Berra, batting .294 with only eighty-eight runs driven in as against one hundred twenty-four the year before, was the first catcher to win the American League award since Mickey Cochrane of Detroit in 1934.

There were bigger and better hitters in the league, according to the official statistics, but Yogi was the most valuable. Ferris Fain of the Athletics, who won the batting crown with a .344 average, placed only sixth in the MVP balloting.

Gus Zernial, lumbering Athletics' outfielder, was RBI leader with one hundred twenty-nine and leading home run producer with thirty-three, but he finished far down in the voting. Even Ted Williams of the Red Sox, with thirty homers and one hundred twenty-six runs, was only thirteenth.

The greatest disappointment was DiMaggio's failure to

break into the scoring for MVP honors, and it was felt this might have had some effect on his decision to retire from baseball.

Berra found it difficult to believe that DiMag wouldn't be with the Yankees when the 1952 season started. "I'm not giving up on Joe so quick," Yogi said. "He says one thing now, another day it could be different. I'll wait till spring training starts. Then we'll know."

More than anyone, Yogi hoped DiMag would return. The burden of the Yankee attack weighed heavily on his shoulders that winter. DiMag was gone . . . Tommy Henrich was gone. . . . It meant he would be moved into the cleanup spot, a pressure he didn't relish.

Yogi worried, too, because he had batted under .300 even while winning the MVP award. In self-analysis, he felt he had departed from his original hitting concept.

"I took too many," he confided to Rizzuto, meaning he let too many balls go by as Stengel had advised. "I used to be a first ball hitter. That's the one I was hitting when I had my .322 year. Next season I'm not laying off the first pitch."

It was still on his mind when Yogi drove in from New York to his job at the Newark clothing store, but the shock of the banner signs with his name and picture emblazoned outside the establishment erased all other thoughts.

The place was mobbed with well-wishers, gawkers and customers. Yogi never wrote so many orders or went through the motions of fitting so many purchasers as he did that night. The store officials beamed and Rizzuto was as happy as if he himself were raking in the profits.

"This is just the beginning," Phil chortled *sotto voce* during a break. "Wait'll you see what's lined up for you on TV and endorsements . . . man, oh, man!"

Berra, normally shy about speaking engagements, began

to find himself more at ease in front of an audience. He never went alone, depending on Jackie Farrell of the Yankee staff or Rizzuto to boost his morale.

Rizzuto had done a great deal for Berra since they had been roommates two years ago. There was a feeling of kinship which went even deeper than the fact that both were of Italian extraction. They understood each other without uttering a word. A true bond existed between these two poor boys who had struggled upward on their baseball talents.

At first, when Stengel put them together, Phil lectured Yogi on baseball, taught him how to dress and act properly and how to conduct himself in the new world which had opened for the kid from The Hill.

He showed Yogi how to handle the fans, how to comport himself in the hotel dining rooms, how to act with the press. But above all, he was a friend. They became inseparables.

Rizzuto even tried to wean Yogi away from comic books. The little shortstop picked out novels for Yogi occasionally and introduced him to some of the better detective fiction authors. Dutifully, Yogi read the books Phil set out and learned to enjoy them.

It was Rizzuto who was instrumental in getting the Berras to move east, not only for the immediate financial gain but for the long-range benefits in every direction. With the birth of his second son, Timothy, Yogi had to think about schools and community life for his growing family.

In 1952 he started spring training earlier than ever before. Again Yogi voiced doubts about Stengel's advice to wait out the pitchers.

"Everybody kept after me last spring to get walks, walks, walks," Berra said. "They told me if I quit hitting at bad balls, I'd draw seventy or eighty walks and force the pitchers to give me good stuff to hit at."

Yogi took a few practice belts and resumed. "So I got fifty-two walks and what was my average? A measly .294, not nearly as good as the year before with .322. My RBI's dropped, too."

He rolled his eyes in disgust.

"Unless Casey lays down the law and makes me hold off on those outside balls, I'm gonna forget about walks and concentrate on getting hits. I haven't got camera eyes like Ted Williams."

Mickey Mantle, walking by, caught the last part of Yogi's monologue. "What do you call a good ball to hit, Yogi?" he asked.

"Anything that comes within six inches of the plate and no more than six inches over my head," Berra answered quickly. "They say I go for pitches a foot over my head, but that's the bunk."

"Depends on the size of your head," someone cracked. It was a gentle needle for a crack Berra was supposed to have made when he was being fitted for a cap.

"What size?" the equipment man had asked and Yogi replied: "Ya mean now or when I'm in condition?"

There was sound reasoning behind Yogi's intention to return to his old style of hitting.

"Look, the pitchers got smart on me," he argued. "They knew I was laying off and snuck the good ones in. All I know is I struck out seventeen times last year and only twelve in 1950."

Part of the blame for his batting sag, Berra felt, was on the heavy work load, particularly in double-headers. "I caught one hundred forty-one games," he said. "That's okay. All I ask is for Casey to let up on using me twice in one day."

It was just after lunch. Berra and some of the other Yankees were lolling around on the grass, soaking up sunshine.

"Doesn't this feel good?" Rizzuto yawned. He was lying prone, face up to the skies. It was peaceful and relaxed before the afternoon drill resumed. Only Berra seemed to have firecrackers in him.

"What's eating you?" Lopat asked. "Relax. I thought you're the guy who beefed about working too much."

"Only double-headers," Yogi explained. "I wanna get out and hit against some of you lefties today. They give me a couple of headaches last year."

Lopat chewed reflectively on a blade of grass. "Yeah, maybe so," he said slowly. "But you sure gave some of them headaches, too."

By early March, Stengel announced that Berra would be his cleanup hitter, the man to take over now that DiMaggio was gone. It wasn't a popular move with Yogi.

"I don't wanna hit fourth," he had told Casey in September when DiMag had dropped out of the number four spot. "I don't hit good there. I tighten up. Let me bat lower down, fifth or someplace."

Fighting to keep the Yankees in first place at the time, Stengel ignored his backstop's request and Berra went into a batting dive. Finally, Casey had to revise his batting order.

Now it was a matter of convincing Berra that he could fill the role. The old persuading job was on again, with Casey publicly praising Yogi on every possible occasion. But the catcher remained doubtful.

"I don't know," he said with obvious concern. "If I'm half as good as Casey says I'll be satisfied."

Meanwhile Stengel was seeking the proper replacement for DiMag in both center field and in the batting order. He had Mantle, Jackie Jensen and Bob Cerv, a husky rookie.

When the Grapefruit Circuit opened on March 8th against the Cardinals, Stengel had Berra hitting fourth, with Jensen, Bauer and Joe Collins behind him and Gil McDougald in the number three slot.

"Let's find out who's got what," Casey grunted. "I want a sure hitter in cleanup. The pitchers have to respect the guy."

The experiment with McDougald third in the order and Berra fourth clicked, much to Yogi's surprise and Stengel's gratification.

Within a week, Yogi's qualms began to disappear. He was clouting the ball and happy as nothing else could make him. After whacking a double and single and drawing two passes in a 6–5 triumph over the Dodgers in a night exhibition at Miami, Berra was convinced.

"I didn't like to hit fourth," he admitted to Roy Campanella, the Brooklyn catcher, who had won the National League MVP award in 1951, "but maybe I was just being a little superstitious."

"You over it now?" Campy asked with a smile.

"Sure, it's malarkey," Yogi said disdainfully. "Casey's been telling me about the money I can get hitting fourth."

The statistics for the first seven games told the story better. The Yanks had won six of them and Yogi was batting .318, with seven runs batted in.

The figures were even more telling after Berra was forced out of action with a badly sprained ankle playing against the Dodgers on March 15th. At first it was feared he had suffered a fracture and Stengel turned pale.

Yogi didn't work out again until March 24th, by which time the Yankees had lost five out of their next eight games. A twelve-inning 4–0 loss to the Phillies was the clincher as far as Berra's value to the team was concerned.

No sooner did he return to active duty than misfortune

overtook him again. Playing in an exhibition game at Atlanta on April 4th, Yogi bruised his left wrist so severely that he didn't get into action again until the tenth game of the regular season.

Everything seemed to be working against the Bombers in the spring of 1952. Injuries were frequent and widespread. Stengel constantly had to fill in at positions all through the line-up. Joe Collins and Billy Martin, cocky young infielder, had been side-lined since March.

Bobby Brown, a full-fledged doctor now, was due to enter the service as a navy medico at any moment, and Gerry Coleman was set for duty as a flier for the Marines by June 1st. Stengel shifted rookies and veterans and casualties around like a chess master, striving to keep the Yankees afloat.

The strain was telling, however, and even the good-humored manager began to snap at the newspapermen. Berra was the key, Casey insisted, and when the catcher returned to the line-up on April 28th, he said, "Yogi tells me his hand is all right. I'm taking him at his word and putting him in that fourth slot against all sorts of pitching."

Casey hunched forward, dug his hands into the back pockets of his uniform and scowled.

"The other guys I've tried there haven't delivered. It's no secret. I think Yogi can sock like DiMaggio did—and if he does we'll start moving."

He paused and bitterly contemplated the clouded sky. "It's up to him now," Stengel said, turning away brusquely and walking off.

The greatest pressure of his career was on Berra now and the twenty-seven-year-old catcher knew it only too well.

· 14 ·

"Push-button manager!" Casey Stengel snorted in disgust. "Where are the buttons?"

He spread his hands wide in helpless appeal. The bold gray eyes stared at his dugout visitors before casting a despairing glance heavenward. "I'm losing all my buttons to the horse doctors and the generals and the admirals. I got nothin' to push."

No one laughed. They knew what was eating the cagey Yankee manager. No punch in the line-up, and minus punch the Bombers were just another ball club. And all the jealous sniping about Stengel being a winner only because he had the material gnawed at him, too.

"Look at Yogi," he went on bitterly, gazing toward the batting cage where Berra waited to take his pregame swats. "The long layoff has cut him down. He's gotta start busting some soon. . . ." Casey didn't have to add, "or else."

Yogi's wrist injury kept him out of the first nine league games and when he finally did return he was rusty. The Yankees were staggering, and Stengel experimented daily with new line-ups, searching for a combination which would supply power at the plate.

In eleven games since his return, Yogi collected only nine hits for a shabby .220 average. He had driven in three measly runs and listed two extra base blows, a homer and double.

"I dunno," Yogi muttered humbly when asked why he wasn't hitting. The wrist still bothered him, but he had been hurt before and managed to connect. Now he wasn't even getting wood on the ball.

Dickey watched Berra flounder but said nothing. Stengel was silent. Rizzuto consoled his friend but did not advise. No one rode Yogi, but feeling the weight of all those eyes and hopes on him, he curled up inside.

By May 19th, the Yankees were a lone game above .500 and apparently easy marks for all the right-handed pitchers in the American League. Eleven of their losses had been to starboard hurlers. Twelve of their fourteen wins had been earned against lefties.

The one-two punch Stengel counted on with Gil Mc-Dougald batting third and Berra fourth had fizzled. Gil was hitting .238 and Yogi .258. Berra, who should have been massacring righties, had trouble against any sort of pitching.

The time had come for a heart-to-heart talk, Casey decided.

"How can we help you?" he asked Berra bluntly. "Want to let us go over your batting style? Maybe take some moving pictures?"

Yogi hung his head dejectedly. "Anything you say, Casey," he replied. "All I wanna do is hit." He rubbed a hairy arm across his brow.

"It just don't figure," he rambled on. "I feel good. I see the ball good. I swing good. But I don't connect good."

Stengel tugged his lip and studied his catcher speculatively for a few moments. "I got an idea," he said finally. There was something in his tone that stimulated hope in Berra.

"We been studying you," Stengel continued. "You're pressing . . . pressing so much you're way up front in the batter's box. Did you know that?"

It hadn't occurred to Yogi. "Yeah," he said, suddenly eager. "That's right. I'm crowding the pitchers."

Casey nodded. "Another thing," he said. "You're hitting everything the same way and to the same spot."

He paused as Berra eyed him curiously.

"Know why?" the manager asked. "Same reason. You're up front too far and hitting too soon. You're slapping every pitch down to the right."

Without letting anyone in on it, Stengel and Dickey quietly changed Berra's stance and position at the plate. They moved him back a bit in the box. The idea was to break up the infield defenses, which were playing him heavily on the first base side of the diamond.

The fear that the new stance might cut down distance on Yogi's drives didn't materialize. His bat began to boom. He walloped homers eleven and twelve to help beat the Tigers, 8–0, behind Allie Reynolds' tight hurling June 19th.

His resurgence seemed to buoy the entire club. Everyone began to hit the ball. The Yankees won eleven of thirteen games on that spree and pulled out to a two and one-half-game lead over the Red Sox for first place. While his .263 average still wasn't impressive, Yogi could be proud of his thirty-one RBI's and the timeliness of his base hits.

"A few more games and you'll find me in the three hundreds," he chattered gaily.

It had been a wonderful reversal of form for the Yankees, who were in fifth place, three and one-half games behind Cleveland, at the start of June.

"We're red hot again," Casey told Dickey out of the corner of his mouth, throwing in a wink, "and there's the guy who did it." He pointed to Berra, jabbering with his teammates and carefree as a kindergarten kid again.

"He don't know it," Casey confided, "but he's our cleanup man the rest of the way."

The New York club opened a four-game gap over Boston by July 25th, with Yogi's twenty-one homers leading the league.

Stengel's quips, edgy when the Yankees lost and whimsical when they won, were the best indicators of the relaxed mood. "That Yogi," he told reporters one day in a tone which combined the elements of awe and marvel, "coulda been a great outfielder. But he wanted to be a catcher. Know why? 'Cause in the outfield he wouldn't have anyone to talk to," Casey guffawed. He could afford to laugh. The Yankees were knocking off the contenders one by one, fastening a firm grip on first place.

The Indians surged back in August, only one game off the pace when they rolled into the Bronx for a series with the Bombers. The Yankees' comfortable lead had dwindled drastically with three straight defeats by the White Sox.

Cleveland moved to first place on August 22nd by beating the Yankees, 6–4, behind Mike Garcia, but didn't stay there long. Raschi turned on the screws with a one-to-nothing shutout the next day and the Bombers were on top again.

The Yankees knocked the Tribe out of the race on September 14th in sweltering Municipal Stadium before seventy-three thousand partisan fans.

Even Yogi, the boy from St. Louis, found the heat oppressive as the Yankees prepared to face Garcia, a twenty-game winner with a string of twenty-eight scoreless innings and four straight decisions over the New Yorkers.

Casey banked on Ed Lopat, a control southpaw, but he

took no chances. "The first hint you get he's weakening," the manager warned Berra, "gimme the sign."

He had nothing to worry about. Lopat, refreshed by an extra night's rest in Cleveland before the rest of the team arrived, handled the Tribe like babes in the woods.

Berra almost punctured Garcia's scoreless skein in the second inning but overdid his bellywhopping act. He was safe at second on a face-first slide after the Indians first sacker mishandled his grounder and threw carelessly.

Mantle, up next, bunted, and Yogi, sprinting recklessly, dove for third like a football tackler. He beat Easter's throw from across the diamond but the slide was too dynamic. Yogi couldn't apply the brakes, skidded past the sack and was tagged out by Al Rosen.

A grimly determined Berra made up for it with good measure in the next inning. Lopat opened the frame with a double to center, reached third on Rizzuto's single and scored when Joe Collins slammed a shot off Bobby Avila's glove.

Mantle tried a two-strike bunt which Garcia managed to shovel to Birdie Tebbets for an out at the plate, but Woodling walked to fill the bases when Berra came up again.

Tebbetts, the big Cleveland catcher, greeted him like a long-lost friend. "Good to see ya up here," he bantered. "You're always good for an out."

"I had my out," Yogi shot back. "Not my fault if your guy over there"—nodding toward Easter on first—"couldn't make it stick. Now I gotta get my hit!"

He watched the first pitch whistle by for a strike and the next two go for balls. Garcia had to come in with something around the plate, Yogi figured. He tightened his grip and waited.

Big Mike tried his fast ball, shoulder high and tight.

Berra slashed it down the first base line past the bag and into right field. It was a clean single, scoring Collins and Mantle.

With Early Wynn hurling in the ninth, Berra singled in another run and the game ended in a 7–1 Yankee win.

Ten days later Berra hammered a double and a single as the Bombers buried the Red Sox, 3–2, in Boston for Allie Reynolds' twentieth win of the season. The race was over.

Winning a fourth straight pennant was a sparkling achievement for Stengel in view of the handicaps and misfortunes blocking his way. The Korean conflict had stripped the team of Gerry Coleman, Bobby Brown and Tom Morgan.

DiMaggio's retirement had left a gaping void and a pre-season shoulder injury to Lopat, a twenty-one-game winner the year before, created additional problems. But Stengel juggled his players with masterful artistry to extract the most out of the men available.

Although Berra's .273 batting average was not prepossessing in any sense, the cold statistics alone could not provide a true evaluation of his worth to the club. His ninety-eight runs batted in, his thirty homers and his great performance behind the plate told the story better.

Berra's thirty circuit blows established a new Yankee record for catchers. Until this time, Bill Dickey's twenty-nine four-baggers hit in 1927 was the top homer mark for a backstop on the New York club.

The Brooklyn Dodgers won the race in the National League after a rough time with the Giants. The new star in Flatbush was Joe Black, strapping twenty-eight-year-old right-handed fireball pitcher who worked fifty-six games and emerged with a 15–4 record.

It was Black who started for Chuck Dressen in the 1952 World Series opener at Ebbets Field, defeating Reynolds in a 4–2 duel. Jackie Robinson and Duke Snider poled homers off Reynolds, while PeeWee Reese smashed one off reliever Ray Scarborough.

In the dressing room underneath the Ebbets Field stands after the game, the Yankees berated themselves for their playing that afternoon. "Six hits!" Billy Martin, the young second baseman, exploded in disgust and anger.

"That fella was pitching hard," Stengel admitted, "but we shoulda got to him."

Sipping a soda, Yogi relaxed glumly in front of his dressing bin. Reynolds walked by on his way to the shower and slapped the catcher fondly across the shoulders.

Yogi looked up apologetically. "Sorry, Chief," he said. "We couldn't get you the runs."

"We'll get 'em tomorrow," vowed McDougald. Gil had homered in one run and Woodling, pinch-hitting for Allie, had tripled and scored on Bauer's single.

The Bombers lived up to their word in the second series contest in the Brooklyn ball park. They smashed Carl Erskine, Billy Loes and Ken Lehman for ten hits, while Raschi limited the Dodgers to three safeties in notching a 7–1 triumph.

Yogi felt a lot better after this game. He went two for three and drove in a run. Billy Martin was the big gun, however, sending in four runs on a homer and a single, while Mantle collected three hits and scored twice.

The series returned to the Stadium for the third game and Yogi strutted out like the kid who knows he's supreme on his own block.

"You're finished here," he kidded Campanella as they crossed paths before the game. Yogi looked around at the ball park he knew so well and at the happy, excited throng in the stands. He never felt so confident and secure.

"That ain't what my boys say," Campy grinned back. "We like it here."

Dressen called on Preacher Roe, a wily left-hander, against Lopat for the Yankees. It was a mildly warm day, windless and perfect for control pitchers.

The good feeling grew stronger for Berra as the game progressed. He slammed a homer for a run in the second inning, doubled in the eighth and scored again on Lopat's base hit. Still, the Bombers trailed, 3–2, going into the ninth inning, with one more chance left.

That chance was wrecked in the top of the ninth when everything happened at once to put the goat horns on Yogi. Singles by Reese and Robinson, followed by a double steal, removed Lopat with two out and brought in Tom Gorman, big right-hander with a tricky sinker.

Andy Pafko was up and Berra signaled for a change-up outside. Gorman checked the base runners and then pitched. The ball came in fast and low, then suddenly took off.

The unexpected speed and the break inward caught Yogi by surprise. He felt a stinging pain as the ball glanced off the tip of his glove, caromed off Umpire Larry Goetz and skittered back toward the stands.

Yogi wheeled around, tearing off his mask, but he couldn't spot the ball. "Where is it, where is it?" he yelled frantically.

The roar of the crowd was deafening. He couldn't hear anything shouted on the field. He knew both runners were pounding down the lines for home as he searched for the ball. By the time he got his hands on it, two runs had scored.

That was the ball game. Mize, batting for Gorman, homered in the last half of the ninth, but it wasn't enough. The Dodgers had won, 5–3, and Yogi felt it was his fault.

"The Dodgers must have me in a jinx," he almost cried. It seemed to be true. This was the team which had made life so miserable for Berra in the 1947 World Series.

Queried by newsmen after the game, Yogi shouldered full responsibility for the play. "I knew what was coming," he said. "There was no misunderstanding about the pitch."

Many reporters felt differently about it. They believed Gorman had gotten his signals crossed and that Yogi was caught unawares by the pitch.

Casey shrugged it off. "Yogi didn't know where the ball was," he said. "But what's the difference. They won the game anyway without it. We didn't play good."

Yogi's left index finger was split and swollen. He was worried about getting into the fourth game.

He played all the way, however, catching Reynolds' magnificent four-hit, two-to-nothing shutout. The Yankees reached Black for only four safeties, two by Mize: a homer in the first inning and a double later on.

Mize delivered another homer the next day, but the Dodgers won, 6–5, in eleven innings as Carl Erskine went the entire way against two Yankee pitchers, lanky Ewell Blackwell and Johnny Sain. Yogi's injured finger pained when he swung a bat and he went hitless.

Now it was do or die as the classic returned to Brooklyn and the Yankees responded typically.

After five scoreless frames in the sixth game, Duke Snider broke the ice with a homer off Raschi in the sixth inning, but Berra, ignoring his throbbing, swollen finger, retaliated with a homer off Billy Loes in the seventh. The Yanks added another run in the same stanza on Woodling's single, Loes's balk and Raschi's drive off the pitcher's knee.

Mantle connected for a home run in the eighth, Snider contributed another in the Dodger half of the inning and that was all. The Yankees won, 3–2, and the series was tied with one game left.

The finale was a thriller. Both clubs were weary. Lopat started against Black, but Reynolds, Raschi and finally Bob Kuzava worked for the Yankees before they pulled it out, 4–2, for the world championship.

Woodling homered to put the Bombers ahead, 3–2, in the fifth and Mantle hit one into the stands in the sixth. Mickey added an insurance run in the seventh with a run-scoring single.

Berra went hitless again, but he did his share behind the bat. It was the toughest game he ever had to catch.

"I'm bone tired," he sighed in the clubhouse. The Yankees were a strangely subdued bunch of winners after the victory and Berra was the most exhausted.

"I'll celebrate next week," he said, stretching out on the rubbing table. "Right now, I'm lucky to move."

Then, still trembling with the released tensions, Yogi surprised even himself by saying, "I don't care if I never see another baseball."

· 15 ·

When Casey Stengel said Yogi Berra preferred to be a catcher because it gave him more opportunity to indulge in neighborly patter, the loquacious Yankee pilot wasn't entirely facetious.

While no chatterbox behind the plate, Yogi was friendly and so good natured that a batter felt guilty if he didn't say a few words, and no umpire could remain taciturn behind Berra.

Strangely, such a genuine aura of amiability and lack of malice surrounded Berra that almost everyone in baseball responded to it. Even the case-hardened umpires fell under Yogi's artless spell.

There was Cal Hubbard, a former All-America football tackle with a massive dignity that could scare most baseball players, who succumbed with the others to Berra's innocent charm.

One day when Hubbard was working behind the plate, a pitch just missed a corner and Cal called it a ball.

Yogi stood still for a moment, the ball nestled in his mitt, and without turning around said, "You missed it, Hub. It was a strike."

The next pitch whanged in and Hubbard said: "Ball two."

This time Yogi shook his head sadly, "Lookit, Hub," he moaned, holding his glove where the ball was supposed to have gone, "right in la bonza."

Deliberately, Hubbard removed his mask and planted his two hundred and seventy pounds over Berra, upon whom he cast a baleful glare.

"Yogi," he intoned sternly, "there's no point in both of us umpiring this game. I have to stay here, but you don't. One more word on balls and strikes and out you go."

"Gee, Hub," Yogi said in an aggrieved tone, "don't get so mad. After all, you can tell when I'm *ferocious*."

Berra meant *facetious* and even Hubbard's judicial mien cracked into a delighted grin.

Most of Yogi's chatter was small talk, ranging from inquiries about health or family to idle comments on the crowd or weather. Ballplayers' humor is rough but the men in the game understand and can take it.

Yogi, like his colleagues, was not averse to digs of a more personal nature when dissatisfied with an umpire's decision. Hubbard pointedly was told that too many fullbacks ran over him in his grid days. Or Larry Napp, associated with the ring as a referee, was politely asked if he caught too many punches. Hank Soar, another former pro football player, got the one about "line-bucking without a helmet."

The umpires, for the most part, didn't mind the griping or wry insults if they weren't overt. The worst offense a catcher could commit was to turn around to protest. The very act of turning brought the fans' attention to the arbiters in a critical way.

Before Yogi learned to keep his nose pointed toward center field while "digging" an ump, he would turn even for casual conversations. If the umps didn't mind, the opposing managers did and they would howl for his ejection.

The batters had a time with Berra, too. Going to the

plate when he caught was an occasion for them. "C'mon, Yogi," some would plead. "Don't talk to me now. Later . . . not now. Lemme hit." Others loved it and Berra sometimes wondered if he wasn't relaxing the rival belters a whit too well.

He didn't try to upset his opponents. He was truly sociable and liked to kid certain players. One in particular was Luke Easter, giant first baseman for the Cleveland Indians, who had enormous feet.

"They're not making the batters' boxes big enough," Yogi told Easter. "You'll never get those scows inside the white lines." Luke got the biggest laugh out of it.

There were other and more useful aspects to Berra's jawing. He had a way with pitchers in the tight spots. He and Dickey agreed there were three kinds of hurlers: Some pitchers had to be babied and when things got tough, some had to be whipped and some could handle the situation nicely by themselves.

Ed Lopat, Allie Reynolds and Whitey Ford never needed anything but a rest when things were going bad. Yogi walked out to the mound trying to stall in order to provide the needed breather.

"That fella always knows what's going on and what he's doin'," Stengel said of Berra.

The matter of how he could best help the Yankees in the hitting department was a source of worry to Yogi. Looking ahead to the 1953 campaign, the catcher saw it as a joint problem for himself and the club.

"What do I do?" he puzzled with Rizzuto one evening during the winter after a stint in the Newark clothing shop. "Go for homers or go for average?"

Little Phil appreciated the astuteness of the question.

"Last season I pulled too much, going for the homer," Berra continued. "I overdid it and in the last month I came up with just two. I wind up with thirty, but I strike out twenty-four times and I hit .273. If I go for average I think I can get up around .322 like in 1950 and maybe even get a chance at the batting title. See, Casey wants me to bunt, like Campy did in the series."

Rizzuto put on a look of mock alarm. "Hey, don't steal my stuff," he implored. "You want me to go for homers and take your bread and butter?"

Berra was anxious to get an early start and a good one that spring.

"I don't know what it is," he told Ed Lopat, a neighbor and golf partner, "but I never had a good spring. Just look at the records and it shows I don't hit early."

"Start in sooner," Ed suggested, but not too seriously because he knew how hard Yogi always tried.

"Now, take the summer," Yogi rambled on. "In the hot weather I'm in there socking. You'd think it would be tougher."

"You must have that St. Louis blood," Lopat said, thinking how hot that city could be in midsummer.

Berra obviously knew himself perfectly, because in that 1953 season he got off to a dismal start, possibly the worst of his career. At the end of April, Yogi was hitting .208 and he dipped to .188 within a week.

Stengel wasn't too seriously concerned because by this time the Yankees were out in front in the American League race and showing every indication of staying there permanently.

Yogi's left forearm was nicked by Maury McDermott in Boston on May 9th and he didn't return to regular service again until May 21st. There was more than the arm bothering Yogi. An intestinal virus had debilitated him so that his weight was down to one hundred and eighty from his normal one hundred and ninety-four pounds.

It was so bad that secretly Berra bedded down in the hospital each night even though he was in uniform for each game. He never felt worse in his life, Yogi grieved. He was weak, slow and pepless.

But the Yankees started an eighteen-game winning streak and Yogi began the long-awaited upturn in batting on May 27th. He still wasn't fully recuperated from the stomach ailment and on June 2nd he developed a sore arm which hindered him for a few more days.

"Boy, my bat feels heavy," Yogi complained. "Funny thing is that I'm using a thirty-three-ouncer when I usually go for a thirty-five-ounce stick."

Whitey Ford clucked in mocking sympathy. "You poor, poor boy."

Yogi paid no attention. "Look how skinny I am . . . only one hundred and eighty pounds. My uniform's falling off."

"Use adhesive tape," someone suggested.

The Yankees could safely kid Berra now because patently he was out of danger. Since his return to the line-up he had eleven hits in twenty-nine times at bat, bringing his average up to .239. It hadn't been a joking matter before.

Yogi's crowning moment came on June 14th in a double-header sweep at Cleveland before seventy-four thousand spectators. He drove in four runs in the 6–2 opener and two more in the 3–0 nightcap and by nightfall his batting mark was .245.

"Well," gloated Casey, "that ends one worry anyway."

Yogi caught the entire All-Star game at Crosley Field in Cincinnati but went hitless as the National League walloped the American League, 5–1, for its fourth win in a row.

At this point the Bombers had been in a tail spin, with a string of nine straight defeats starting from June 21st. Their lead shrunk drastically until the Yankees snapped out of it with a double win in Chicago.

By mid-August it was rolling again for Berra and the Bombers. His twenty-third homer of the campaign, a blast into the right center field bleachers over four hundred feet from the plate, beat the Senators, 2–0, and extended his own hitting spree to ten straight games.

August had always been his best homer-hitting month and September his worst. It was a mystery no one could fathom, least of all Yogi.

"Maybe I try too hard," he suggested to Mize, the man with the finest hitting form in baseball.

"Can't figure it," Big Jawn conceded grudgingly. "You hit the same. Maybe you just get tired after all those double-headers through the summer."

"This year," Berra vowed, "it's gonna be different. I feel it in my bones."

There was a general laugh. "Which bones . . . the ones in your head?" someone asked.

"You had thirty homers last year," Raschi said. "What'd you hit in September?"

Yogi gave him a dirty look. "That's no way to treat a guy who makes a smart pitcher out of you," he chided.

But Vic insisted. "Give us the figure."

Yogi sighed and lifted up two fingers.

"Two measly, stingy shots," he groaned with bitter memory of his twenty-ninth homer September 1st and not another one for twenty-seven days. "I got number thirty on the last day of the season," he added.

Yogi had little hope of attaining the .328 average or the one hundred and twenty-four RBI's of 1950, but with twenty-three home runs already in the bag by August 23rd he felt it was possible to break his own high mark of thirty.

But the September jinx gripped him as tightly as ever, at least as far as homer clouting was concerned. Try as he might, he hit only four more for a season total of twenty-seven. His final batting average was .296, with one hundred and eight runs batted in, almost phenomenal in view of his terrible start.

"It's aggravating," Yogi admitted with an air of gentle resignation.

"Don't worry, Yogi," consoled Billy Martin. "Maybe you'll be the series hero."

Yogi wielded his bat with greater effect than ever before in a World Series as the Yankees subdued the Brooklyn Dodgers again, four games to two, but it was Billy who emerged with the hero laurels.

A .257 batter that year, Billy the Kid exploded with a record twelve hits for a six-game series, batted .500, clouted two homers, two triples, a double and sent in eight runs.

In contrast, Mickey Mantle was something of a series bust, striking out eight times, although he did wallop two game-winning homers, one a grand slam in the fifth game.

Yogi enjoyed himself thoroughly with nine hits, including a homer and triple, and drove in four runs. In addition, he contributed a couple of fielding gems which choked off a Dodger rally in the series opener at the Stadium.

The Yanks led, 5–4, going into the seventh inning, but the Brooks sailed right into Johnny Sain, relieving Reynolds. Campanella singled, moved to second when Gil Hodges pushed a hit past Rizzuto and scored the tying run on Carl Furillo's line single to center.

Yogi nodded to Stengel, staring at him from the dugout, and Casey signaled to the bull pen to get someone heated up. Billy Cox was up, the Dodger second baseman who had lashed out two hits.

Chuck Dressen decided to outfox the Yankees and Cox surprised everyone by bunting. Surprised everyone but Berra, who pounced on the ball like a tiger. Without a pause or a look, Yogi fired the ball to Gil McDougald on third.

It was an eyelash play as Hodges slid into the bag in a cloud of dust. "Out!" the umpire shouted, and sixty-nine thousand fans roared their appreciation of a beautifully executed play.

Now Clem Labine, third Dodger pitcher of the day, came up to the plate. Again it was a bunt, laid perfectly down the first base line. And again Berra was on it in a flash, with one fluid motion scooping it up and pegging to third.

"Out!" the umpire bawled as McDougald slapped the ball on Furillo in an even closer play.

When Junior Gilliam clipped a foul pop high behind the plate, Yogi was under it for the third out. He trotted into the dugout to enthusiastic applause.

The Yankees won that game, 9–5, and went on to capture the World Championship for their fifth straight year, an unprecedented feat in major league annals.

"This is getting to be a wonderful habit," Yogi grinned the day he picked up a check for $8,280.68, the largest winners' shares in series history.

Then, carefully folding the check into his wallet, Yogi said, "I don't know what I'd do without it."

It was only a pleasantry, but the little catcher was to find out the sad answer in 1954, the year the Yankees lost the pennant.

· 16 ·

Inevitably, when the discussion came around to catchers baseball people found themselves arguing the relative merits of Yogi Berra of the Yankees versus Roy Campanella of the Dodgers.

It was natural, since here were the two standout backstops of their era. Both were sluggers, spirited competitors and superb receivers playing on the top quality teams in their respective leagues.

But if opinion was divided, it was in Yogi's favor. In batting the topic around, most ballplayers preferred him.

"Berra don't strike out as much," a pitcher offered in a chilly-day conclave around the electric heater one leaden afternoon in St. Petersburg in the spring of 1954. "Campy," the speaker continued, "fans twice as much as Yogi and he hits into a lot more double plays."

"They've both been up about the same time," someone else chimed in. "Let's see . . . Yogi's in the majors seven years, Campy six . . . what're they hitting?"

The figures were dug up and Berra showed a five-point advantage over the Brooklyn catcher in lifetime batting.

"There's not much difference up at the plate," another said. "It shows here both've been over .300 twice and knocked in over one hundred runs twice."

"Yeah?" questioned a National Leaguer, "what about homers? Roy's got Yogi beat there."

He flinched at the disgusted glances directed his way. "How do you compare homers," he was razzed, "in two different parks like the Stadium and that bandbox Ebbets Field?"

It was pointed out that while Campy never had a distinguished World Series, Yogi posted a .429 average in the last classic and had done a consistently brilliant backstopping job.

"Can Campy get out after those bunts like Yogi?" the question arose. Everyone agreed Berra was the fastest and the most accurate in the majors on that play. "He's got the reflexes and the speed," the pitcher said. "And a real head for the right pitch. All I know is, I never shake the guy off."

A veteran coach brought out another point. "Yogi's faster on the bases, too. That's why you can bat him third or fourth while Campy's lower down in the order. Yogi can travel. He's no automatic out on the double-play situation."

Cold reality crept into the discussion when a comparison of salaries was suggested. "That's what really counts," the coach said. "The bank roll average."

Berra's 1954 contract settled in late January, called for forty-two thousand dollars. Campanella was receiving thirty-five thousand dollars after a huge pay increase for winning the MVP in 1953. "No contest," someone murmured and the confab broke up in laughter.

The 1954 season was a peculiar and disappointing one to the Bombers, who won one hundred and three games yet wound up eight games behind the pennant-clinching Cleveland Indians, who rolled up one hundred and eleven victories.

It was a spirited race, with New York only three and one-half games off the Tribe as late as September 5th, but the

Yankees blew whatever chance they had in dropping a twin bill in Cleveland against Bob Lemon and Early Wynn.

Although the Bombers led the league in batting, with a team average of .268 and four men above the .300 mark— Irv Noren, Andy Carey, Mickey Mantle and Berra—age and a weakened pitching staff finally caught up with them.

Phil Rizzuto, thirty-six years old and obviously slower, emerged with a dismal .195 in batting. The Scooter even tried wearing glasses in action in a desperate effort to regain his old form.

A pair of youngsters performed the heavy chores for the mound staff. Rookie Bob Grim won twenty games and Whitey Ford took sixteen, while veterans Reynolds and Lopat won thirteen and twelve, respectively.

That the Yankees won as many as one hundred and three games could be credited in good part to the slugging of Berra and Mantle. Yogi whacked twenty-two homers, batted in one hundred and twenty-five runs and hit .307. Mickey poled twenty-seven homers, drove in one hundred and two runs and batted an even .300.

Yogi enjoyed the greatest All-Star game performance in his six appearances in the midseason classic. He got two hits and caught the whole show as the American Leaguers snapped their jinx and outblasted the National Leaguers, 11–9, in vast Municipal Stadium at Cleveland.

This was the game in which Stan Musial got the last word at bat but Yogi got the last out.

It was the end of the ninth, the American League ahead, 11–9, with Virgil Trucks of Detroit pitching and two out. Duke Snider of the Dodgers worked Trucks for a pass and up came the ever-dangerous Musial.

It was growing dark and the sixty-eight thousand fans in the stands and countless millions of television viewers fretted with nervous excitement.

Musial represented the potential tying run and Stan the Man was just the lad to accomplish it. He came up to the plate narrow eyed with determination, his whole being concentrated on the pitch.

"Stan," said Yogi as he signaled for the pitch, "where'll we meet for dinner tonight?"

"At Cavioli's, eight o'clock," Musial spat out of the side of his mouth as Trucks let loose.

Musial swung, the ball bounded harmlessly down the first base line to Mickey Vernon of the Senators and the game was over.

The season was full of high spots for Berra. There was the night Yogi was able to "do something" for Johnny Sain, a pitcher Berra deeply admired. Sain was a real pro who filled a mighty, but unsung, role in the bull pen.

To Yogi, who found it a pleasure to catch, there was a certain injustice in Sain doing such a great amount of relief hurling without commensurate credit in the win column.

"Gotta do something for that guy," Yogi would say. "If there was some way. . . ."

The "way" appeared one night early in the season in Chicago. Sain had been called into the game in the eighth inning before the Yankees, trailing by a run, tied it up.

Now it was the ninth inning, with Don Johnson pitching for the White Sox. He walked shortstop Willie Miranda, but whiffed Mantle. Then he walked Noren and the winning run was on second base when Berra picked a bat out of the rack.

With one foot out of the dugout, Yogi turned to Sain, big and calm on the bench. "I'm gonna get you a win," he said and strode to the plate.

Johnson was high for ball one. Manager Paul Richards called time and went out to the mound.

"Nothin'll help, Paul," Yogi advised. Richards ignored him.

Berra fouled off the next pitch. The third was exactly where he wanted it and Yogi leaned into it for a scathing single to center which sent Miranda home. The Yanks won and Sain had his present.

One of the most important developments in Berra's education as a batter was a new-found ability to hit to the opposite field. He resented insinuations in some quarters that it was merely accidental.

"I'm doing it on purpose," he insisted. "They're pitching me outside, so I hit to left. The pitchers don't want me to pull the ball. I tried it a little last year and I like it."

This, plus other Berra feats with the bat, made him the despair of American League twirlers. It was impossible to get a "book" on him because he was liable to wallop any kind of pitch: close, outside, high or low.

An infected finger kept Yogi out of action a few days late in September when the race was over, but he returned on the last day of the season in time for an interesting experiment.

Stengel, shifting his players about with an eye to the future, tried Berra at third base. Yogi fared nicely at the hot corner, handling two chances flawlessly, but he was less than adequate at bat, going hitless in five tries and slamming two double-play balls.

"It's all over," Yogi said slowly, surveying the vast terrain of Yankee Stadium after the game. "I love the joint until I have to hit here."

Hank Bauer, the former Marine who patrolled the outfield for the Yankees, nodded. "I know what you mean," he said. "It's tough on hitters."

"It's that doggoned big outfield," Yogi went on. "Tough

shadows, tough drafts, lots of room for fast flycatchers."
He turned to Hank. "Know my favorite park?"

Bauer waited for the answer. "Detroit. That's the best.
You can see the ball all the time."

"Philadelphia is good."

"Used to be," Yogi cut in, "but not any more for me.
Don't know why, either. I just stopped getting my good
socks there. Chicago and Washington are bad, too."

"Well," Bauer sighed. "No series dough this year.
"Good-by, Stadium. . . ." They walked into the shadows
of the dugout, disappointed gladiators consoled by the
thought that another year beckoned with new opportunity.

But 1954 hadn't revealed all of its surprises for Yogi.
The Baseball Writers Association voted him the Most
Valuable Player of the Amercan League for the second
time in his career.

"I didn't think I'd get it," Yogi said humbly. He almost
didn't, his two hundred and thirty votes barely beating out
two members of the flag-winning Cleveland Indians. Larry
Doby totalled two hundred and ten, Bobby Avila two hundred and three, a fatal split that helped put Berra in.

Yogi was the first MVP repeater since Ted Williams and
the only catcher besides the great Mickey Cochrane singled
out for this honor. Moreover, he had made the top ten in
the balloting five of the last six years, missing out only in
1949.

The brief experiment on third base excited numerous
rumors about Berra's moving out of the backstop post in
1955. Even Yogi thought it possible.

"I'll play anywhere they want if it helps," he said. "I
know I can do good in the outfield. I tried it six years ago.
And I like that third base spot, too."

"What's the difference, eh, Yogi?" his brother John said.
"As long as you get up to hit."

Berra lifted his hands and hunched his shoulders in the universal sign of resigned acceptance. "Like I said, if Casey wants me someplace else, I'll go."

"Who's gonna catch if you don't?" John wanted to know.

Elston Howard, a fine Negro prospect, John was told. "Look, Dickey can teach this kid just like he taught me," Yogi said sensibly. "This Howard can hit, too. We need all the power we can get."

John shook his head sadly. "I dunno . . . what'll that do to your chances for another MVP?"

The question caught Yogi by surprise. He blinked before answering. "I never thought of it that way, Johnny," he began, then paused. Only one Yankee had ever won three MVP designations and that was Joe DiMaggio. The immortal Lou Gehrig had won it twice.

No, it was ridiculous . . . incredible . . . impossible. To himself, Yogi still was the plain-faced, stocky little guy from The Hill. A baseball player, yes. But he had no conception of himself as a DiMaggio!

These were things that happened to other people, not to Lawrence Peter Berra. Still, he *had* won the MVP twice. He was the highest salaried catcher in baseball. Why couldn't he make it a third time? Or maybe more?

"I'm young," he said aloud while John stared at his famous kid brother. "I'm only twenty-nine."

Then, seemingly almost ashamed of the trend of his innermost thoughts, Yogi faced the truth.

"No," he uttered softly. "I gotta play where they need me. It's gotta be where I'm most valuable to the team, not to myself."

He looked at his brother with apologetic eyes. "That's how it is with me," he said.

John put his arm around Yogi's shoulder. He was proud of the kid, prouder than when Yogi won the MVP, but there were words choked in him that he couldn't say.

"You're all right," he said finally. "Yogi, you're all right."

· 17 ·

Casey Stengel poked his head out of the Stadium dugout and squinted into the sun for a better view of Berra in the batting cage.

It was almost time to start the game with the Red Sox and the stands buzzed with the din of fifty thousand chattering, excited baseball fans.

Stengel watched Berra, his practice swings completed, plod back to the dugout, hunched over wearily, his eyes red and heavy. Both hands were taped and sore. His left shoulder was stiff and his back ached. He had fought a virus for four days and a racking cough disturbed his sleep.

Yogi dropped his bat into the rack and flopped down in the corner near the dugout steps. Casey erased the concern from his face and fixed a smile on his lips as he ambled over to the battered catcher.

"How ya feelin', young fella?" he chuckled, throwing a wink to the men on the bench. Yogi's answer was a mute but expressive shrug.

"Gotta ask him these things," Casey said to the dugout in general. "You know, Yogi's got the big in with the bosses."

It was a routine joke in the club, Stengel kidding Berra

because of the catcher's winning ways with the executives during contract time.

"Feel like catchin' today?" Stengel asked, dropping a hand on Yogi's shoulder. "I mean, is it all right with you, Mr. Berra?" He winked again and even Berra grinned.

"Now if you don't," the pixyish manager resumed, "just say so. Of course, if I insist and you tell Mr. Weiss and Mr. Webb and Mr. Topping, I may get fired."

More grins from the players and the newsmen within hearing range.

"But you wouldn't do that, Yogi," Casey said. "Nah, Yogi here might even put some of his money in my bank." Stengel was on the board of a local bank in his home town of Glendale, California.

Later, when Berra was taking his turn in the cage again, Stengel became serious. "Remember when he was considered funny?" he reminisced to a writer. "What's funny about him?"

There was no answer to that and after a brief silence while they watched Yogi smash out a few liners, he spoke again. "The guy's the greatest catcher in baseball, has a good home, a lovely wife and family. He's a big success.

"You gotta be a real man to be a catcher," he continued. "Strong, you know. Just bending down and getting up in that catcher's stuff is tough after nine innings. Look at that guy, all taped and bandaged and hurting. To me—," and Stengel paused for emphasis, his gray eyes glinting—"he's a great man. We're lucky to have him and so are the pitchers."

He walked away for a moment, then drifted back. "I got my ideas on how to pitch to certain hitters in this league, but once in a while Yogi will come over and tell me he thinks I'm wrong and then give me the right slant. So I always tell him okay, do it your way." Stengel cocked his head birdlike, pursed his lips and held still for a moment. "Funny thing," he said, finally, "most of the time he's right!"

Casey was justified in feeling this way about Berra because, sick and battered, his catcher was carrying the club in one of its greatest battles for the pennant.

Bruised, sore, exhausted, Yogi kept on day after day as the Yankees struggled to stay even with the Cleveland Indians and the Chicago White Sox in the summer of 1955.

It had been touch and go all season, with Stengel juggling his players to get the most from a squad incapacitated by injuries and weakened by the retirement of Reynolds and Lopat, which left two gaps in the pitching staff.

At the All-Star game break on July 12th, the Yankees held a fat five-game lead over Cleveland and six over Chicago, but from July 22nd on through to September the race had narrowed until it seemed no team ever could squeeze through.

Now it was September 16th, with the Red Sox in the Stadium and Casey desperate for the victory. Cleveland was a full game ahead of the Bombers. If the gap widened, it might be fatal and forever.

"You think I like to play him," Casey said slowly, watching Yogi walk out to the plate for the first inning. "I gotta use him. What else can I do? He's the guy who's holding us together."

Stengel wiped his arm across his mouth in a nervous motion. "Take him out and we fall apart."

Sick or well, Berra kept on playing. He smashed out hits, he drove in runs, he blocked the plate, he cut down runners on the base paths. He also babied and coaxed and commanded the pitchers, called the signals and never failed in the myriad crises which confronted the Yankees from day to day.

Whitey Ford was pitching for the Bombers against towering Frank Sullivan of Boston. In the fifth inning, with both sides scoreless, Yogi dragged himself to the batter's box with two men out and two on.

The crowd was shouting encouragement, demanding runs, but the noise seemed blurred and far away to tired Yogi. Sullivan threw with a wide, sweeping motion that concealed his fast ball effectively and dangerously. It was easy to be hit by one of his hard-to-follow fast ones.

Yogi leaned forward, swinging the bat. It felt like lead, heavy and lifeless, but he savagely forced his body to respond.

Sullivan whipped over a strike. Berra saw it but never moved a muscle. He was too tired. Dimly, he heard the yells and catcalls from the fans.

The Bosox flinger reared back again and burned in another one, inside and low. Yogi's bat flashed, connected and the ball hummed into the right field stands for his twenty-sixth homer of the year. The blow put the Yankees ahead, 3–0, but Boston made it up in the eighth, chasing Ford.

In the ninth inning, with the score tied and the aging Ellis Kinder on the mound for the Red Sox, Hank Bauer caught one on the nose for a home run and the crowd went wild.

Once again Yogi trudged to the plate, bat in hand. Kinder surveyed the weary figure and decided to steam one past him. It was a mistake. Fatigued though he might be, Berra never could resist a fast ball on the first pitch. Bang! It sailed out to the bleachers in right center and Yogi had number twenty-seven.

The blow sewed up a 5–3 victory and when Cleveland lost out west the Bombers went into first place by two percentage points.

"That's what I mean about Berra," Stengel said in his

office under the stands later to the same baseball writer. "He could be dead, but he still wins 'em for you."

That was the push that sent the Yankees up front for good and they wound up the season three games up on the Indians and five on the White Sox.

Despite his injuries and illnesses in 1955, Yogi caught one hundred and forty games, batted .272, stroked twenty-seven homers and drove in one hundred and eight runs.

The Yankees had two other .300 hitters: Mickey Mantle with .306 and thirty-seven homers and Bill Skowron with .319. But it was Yogi who carried the load and socked the pay-off shots.

Again it was Brooklyn as the National League foe in the World Series, but for once the Yankees faltered. The Dodgers shattered their hex in the fall classic to edge Casey Stengel's team four games to three, with a thrilling finish to climax the series.

The Yankees won the opener at home, 6–5, behind Ford, chiefly on three homers off Don Newcombe which accounted for five runs. Joe Collins, a .234 hitter during the season but a money hitter in the Yankee tradition, clouted two and Elston Howard the other.

Yogi, who collected one hit the first game, got two more in Tommy Byrne's five-hit 4–2 victory in the second contest. The Brooks struck back at Ebbets Field, winning 8–3 as Johnny Podres beat Bob Turley, and 8–5 behind circuit blows by Campanella, Hodges and Snider.

Berra poled a homer in the fifth game, but the Yankees lost, 5–3, as Snider crashed two and Sandy Amoros one. Back in the Stadium, the Yankees evened it up by winning, 5–1, when Ford hurled a four-hitter and Berra went two for three at the plate.

The stage was now set for one of the most dramatic and exhilarating games in World Series history. Podres, brilliant rookie, twirled an eight-hit 2–0 shutout while three Yankee pitchers allowed only five safeties but lost the game.

In the sixth, with the Dodgers leading, Yogi barely missed being the series savior and hero. Martin walked and McDougald bunted to put two men on the bases. Podres, pitching carefully to Berra, kept the ball outside, but Yogi reached out and rifled a fly inside the left field foul line. Amoros raced after the ball in what seemed a hopeless gesture, but the little lefty made a desperate leaping stab to collar it.

Reese, canny Brooklyn shortstop, was in perfect position for the relay, firing the ball to Hodges to double up McDougald. Except for Amoros' great catch, the Bombers would have had two certain runs and the likelihood of more.

Personally, for Yogi this was the finest series performance of his career. The blocky little powerhouse batted .417 on ten hits, but somehow his joy was shadowed.

"What good are the hits if they don't win us the series?" he complained to Rizzuto.

"Who you kidding?" Phil scoffed. "You wouldn't give your grandmother one of those bingles."

"Naw," Yogi insisted. "I'm serious, Phil." He stopped, groping for a way to express his feelings. "I'd give half those hits . . . honest!"

Behind the bantering, everyone in baseball appreciated what Berra meant to the Yankees, so it wasn't surprising that even with his .272 batting average Yogi was the Baseball Writers Association choice for the 1955 Most Valuable Player award.

It had been a closely contested vote, but Berra emerged with two hundred and eighteen ballots as against two hundred and one for Al Kaline, Detroit's .340 outfielder, and two hundred for Al Smith, Cleveland's .306 all-rounder. Ted Williams was fourth with one hundred and forty-three votes and Mickey Mantle fifth with one hundred and thirteen.

The choice of Berra was a sound one. Kaline, for all his value to the Tigers, could not lift them above fifth place. Smith fizzled toward the end and so did the Indians. Williams, great as he was, couldn't lift the Red Sox higher than fourth.

But Yogi, working day after day in baseball's most exacting position, helped push the Yankees to the pennant.

As usual, the news reached him at home. He and Carmen had just tucked their two sons away for the night when the phone rang.

Joe Trimble of the New York *Daily News* almost sputtered in his excitement. "Don't you realize," he shouted, "that you've got the greatest chance to be the first man ever to win four MVP awards?"

"Well," laughed Berra, "I'm sure gonna try."

At the age of thirty, he had won it three times in five seasons with his peak years still ahead of him. Jimmy Foxx became the first three-time winner in 1938 and Joe DiMaggio completed his triple in 1947.

Over in the National League, Roy Campanella was the second triple winner, joining Stan Musial in the charmed circle. It didn't seem strange to Yogi or Roy that catchers had captured the prize in both major leagues.

Meeting in the Associated Press offices at Rockefeller Center, Yogi and Roy stopped stock still and contemplated each other with mock amusement.

"So they snuck you in here to mess up my pictures," Campy said.

"G'wan," Yogi responded, "you're just afraid the photos'll show you up uglier than me."

Underneath the badinage was a solid vein of respect and admiration for each other. These were the two greatest catchers of their generation, men who in future years would be the subjects of countless arguments among baseball fans. Who was the best—Yogi or Campy?

Right now, they were occupied with more mundane concerns.

"I'm waiting for you to sign first," Campy told Berra. "Then I'm gonna ask for more than you get."

Yogi grinned. "That's okay with me," he said, "as long as I get mine. My bosses take good care of me."

It didn't proceed that easily or smoothly for Yogi, however. The Yankees kept their negotiations with the catcher quiet, but it was no secret that Berra was adamant about a fifty-thousand-dollar contract.

In the end, General Manager George Weiss had to accede to Berra's demands, but not before warning that he wasn't too satisfied with the backstop's .272 average.

"Don't work me so hard," Yogi retorted, "in those double-headers in August. Then, maybe you'd see me sock .320 or so."

This wasn't the only money he was earning. He was a national hero, a household byword with a name that meant cash when spelled out by the advertising and business firms.

In addition to numerous speaking engagements and endorsements, Yogi invested wisely in a number of directions. He bought into a bottled soft drink, a chocolate beverage called Yoo-Hoo, and was listed as vice-president of the firm.

After a long search, he and Rizzuto bought ground in Clifton, New Jersey, on which they planned to build a huge million-dollar bowling emporium equipped with cocktail lounge and restaurant. But for all his commercial enterprises, Yogi still was the same modest, unassuming chap who had come up to the Yankees as a pudgy rookie in 1947.

He had traveled a long way since then. The shyness

which had been mistaken for stupidity, the hesitance with strangers and the naïve innocence were gone. He had acquired skills and poise, confidence and directness.

And for the first time since he came up from Newark in 1947, Yogi enjoyed a good spring training season. The Yankees never saw a healthier, sounder, more vigorous Yogi than the one who cavorted at St. Petersburg in 1956.

Berra glowed. His bat rattled off a wicked symphony of base hits. His catching and throwing were superb. He ran the bases like a scared rabbit. And he felt wonderful.

"No bandages, no bruises, no nothin' " he marveled as the Bombers ended their spring exhibition campaign and prepared to open the American League season in Washington.

Berra, a notoriously slow starter, had finished the spring tour with a .304 batting average and his rooters considered this a definite indication that he was headed for the greatest year of his career.

"I don't see why not," Dickey told reporters. "Yogi should hit over .300 every year."

Stengel felt the same way, and being the shrewd manager he was, practiced his own psychology on Berra that spring.

He sidled up to within earshot of Berra and muttered: "Now there's my catcher, all dressed up nice and neat in that white uniform. He likes to stand around the batting cage and yak-yak with the boys—telling 'em about his money, maybe, or what it's like to be vice-president of the Yoo-Hoo company."

It was the big needle wielded by a master, masked by humor but with a most serious intent. What Casey wanted to impress on Yogi was that his perennial spring slumps could be merely a state of mind.

"If that man could get off to a good start," Stengel ranted, "there's no telling how much he'd hit."

The accuracy of the manager's words was evident in Yogi's explosive season debut against the Senators on April 17th before President Eisenhower and the nation's dignitaries.

Yogi enjoyed a perfect day at bat, going four for four, socking a homer and driving in five runs. The Yankees won, 10–4, in a fashion that seemed to foreshadow coming events for the 1956 season.

"Wotta start!" Berra exulted. "I gotta keep it up!"

Whitey Ford snickered. "Sure, you'll wind up batting 1.000 and sending in six hundred runs," the blond pitcher kidded.

"Boy," murmured Gil McDougald, "I can just see Yogi sitting down to talk contract with Weiss. What'll you ask for, Yogi?"

Berra played it dead pan. "Just what I'm worth," he answered. "One million smackeroos."

"That's reasonable," Billy Martin agreed. "Of course, that won't leave much for the rest of us. . . ."

Yogi shrugged. "Look," he said earnestly, "you go hit 1.000 and you'll make a million bucks, too."

Gerry Coleman, dressing near by, looked up at Martin. "This is the guy they called dumb?" he asked wryly. "I should be so dumb the rest of my life."

· 18 ·

Paul Richards, the tall, astute manager of the Baltimore Orioles, settled back in his chair in the office of the visiting team's dressing room under the Yankee Stadium.

"When you get to the seventh inning," he said sharply, "the most dangerous hitter in baseball is Yogi Berra."

He could appreciate this anew after Baltimore's 8–6 defeat by the Bombers. It had been Yogi's long single in the fifth that scored Mickey Mantle to tie it at five-all and his homer in the seventh to knot it up at six-all again, before Mantle chased two runs across in the eighth to ice the game.

It was the middle of May and the Yankees had taken the league lead for good. Berra was hitting .336 and he had eleven home runs. He was up to .353 a week later when, reaching for a high pitch by Bob Turley in Chicago, he pulled a muscle in his right side.

It was the first time he was side-lined that year and Yogi was disconsolate. "Something had to happen to spoil it for me," he moaned in the clubhouse.

But if he felt bad, Stengel felt worse. Berra was his steady punch as the rest of the Yankee attack sputtered and stalled. What Casey feared most was that any prolonged absence from action would cool off Berra's hot bat.

Yogi was gloomier than any of the Yankees had ever

seen him. It wasn't a particularly bad injury, but the doctors regarded it dangerous for him to start playing until it was completely healed.

"I sneezed this morning," Yogi told Rizzuto, "and the pain sent me clear to my knees."

He finally returned to action on May 30th in Washington, where the Yankees won a double-header and the catcher regained his batting eye in the nightcap with two hits.

By June 22nd the Yankees' five-game lead dwindled to one, but they went on an eighteen-game winning streak which tore the league race apart.

Even the scare, when Berra's fingers were smashed by a foul tip off Ted Kluszewski's bat in the All-Star game in Washington, couldn't faze the Yankees after that. Casey seemed angrier about losing 7–6 to the National Leaguers again than worried over Yogi, who had garnered two hits in two times at bat before the accident.

The rest of the 1956 campaign was more a duel between Berra and the .300 mark. After sagging off badly, his bat was ringing again. He socked the two hundred thirty-seventh homer of his career on September 14th for a new major league record for catchers.

Near the end of September, with the pennant clinched, Stengel offered to rest him. "But he don't want it," Casey despaired. "He's too anxious to hit."

The next best thing, Stengel reasoned, was to shift Yogi to an outfield post. "You want to bat?" the manager told Berra. "Okay, play the outfield."

The move gave the Yankees a chance to work Elston Howard behind the plate. It pleased Berra, too.

"It's a breeze out there," he said, "except for the mosquitoes. They're bigger than the ones we got over in New Jersey." This was up in Boston, where the Yankees lost a

13–7 game to the Red Sox with a makeshift club. Stengel was resting all his regulars.

"I don't want to go into a World Series with Mantle and Bauer and Noren crippled like last year," he said.

Yogi knocked in his one hundredth run of the season in the first inning and clouted a double to stretch his consecutive game hitting streak to eighteen. The RBI was also the one thousandth of his major league lifetime.

The season ended in a splurge of homers by the Yankees, Mantle winding up with fifty-two, Berra with thirty and Bill Skowron with twenty-three. Mickey won the triple crown, leading the league in batting, homers and runs batted in.

As a team, the Yankees clouted a league record of one hundred ninety circuit blows, won the pennant by nine games over Cleveland and went into the 1956 World Series against the Dodgers in powerhouse style.

Yogi's .298 average was a disappointment, in a sense, but coupled with his other slugging achievements it represented notable value.

"Stop grumbling," Martin told Berra. "You're still the cleanup hitter, aren't you? And those are the guys who get the big pay."

His grumblings mounted after the Yankees dropped the series opener, 6–3, at Ebbets Field. Sal Maglie, crafty thirty-nine-year-old hurler, tied the Bombers in knots after a shaky first inning marked by Mantle's homer with one on.

At home that night, Yogi sat staring at the blank TV screen. The best thing about a New York–Brooklyn Series was the fact that he could drive home to the Jersey suburbs every night.

"It's no use fretting," Carmen consoled, rumpling his thin hair. "You'll hit tomorrow."

"I could've won it for us today," Yogi despaired, gazing

into the dusk. "I didn't get a hit in three chances. . . ." He banged his fist into a pillow angrily.

"Tomorrow," Carmen murmured softly, "tomorrow you'll hit."

The next day dawned bright and clear with a slight tang in the air. Driving to Flatbush, hundreds of fans waved to Yogi along the way. The cop on the George Washington Bridge gave his best wishes.

"I'm a Dodger fan myself," the officer said, sticking his head out of the change booth, "but I have to go with the man who gives us his steady business, so I hope you get a couple of good belts today."

Don Newcombe, the strapping speedball artist, was on the mound for Brooklyn against Don Larsen of the Yankees. "I like to hit Newk's speed," Berra told Mc-Dougald.

The first time up, with Slaughter on via a single, Yogi walked and Collins whacked in a run with a one-bagger.

Newk was blazing the ball in. "Don't get too close," the bench jockeys shouted as the Bombers came up for the top of the second.

Martin razzed back with a Bronx cheer, then outraced a hit to the infield. Coleman sacrificed and Larsen singled to right field, sending Billy the Kid home. McDougald singled, Slaughter grounded into a force play and Mantle walked, filling the bases.

Berra ambled to the plate as the fans roared. They sensed something special developing in the confident manner with which he settled into the batter's box. Even Campy, who usually had a remark for Yogi, said nothing this time.

Newcombe, taut and angry, hurled the first pitch in like a bullet, high and inside for a ball. Yogi never budged as the pitch whizzed by his cap. He gripped his bat tighter and waited.

Newk checked the bases and then pitched. The ball was a line of white as Yogi swung. Crack! The ball sailed on and on, over the right field barrier and out of the park. A grand slam homer!

It was Yogi's seventh World Series homer and the fifth grand slammer in the entire history of the baseball classic.

That finished Newcombe, but it didn't finish the Dodgers, who bounced back with six runs—in their half of the same inning—all unearned following Collins' error at first base—and went on to win, 13–8. It was an incredible, amazing comeback and sent Brooklyn fans into a frenzy.

"The Yankees are dead . . . finished . . . through," they chanted hysterically outside the ball park. Inside the dressing room, the sobered Bombers heard the shouting.

"Okay, they win two on us and get a head start," Stengel conceded. "But now we're going back to our park. I'm starting Whitey Ford tomorrow and he'll stop 'em."

On a bench in the dressing room, Yogi seethed. He had gone two for four, driven in four runs and made ten put-outs, all for naught. He wasn't thinking of himself or his achievements.

"Whitey," he said to Ford, "we've got to take care of these Dodgers tomorrow."

They did.

Ford scattered eight hits before a throng of 73,977 in the Stadium as the Yankees beat Roger Craig and Clem Labine to win, 5–3. Berra again went two for four, with a double that sent in a run. Slaughter's home run with two on in the sixth off Craig put the Bombers ahead for good.

The Yankees evened the series with a 6–2 triumph in the fourth game as Mantle and Bauer each homered with men on and Berra singled a man home.

There was a slight nip in the air for the fifth game at the Stadium, but the skies were clear and the huge ball park windless. Don Larsen, the big, rawboned right-hander who had changed to a "no windup" style midway in the season, was slated to hurl against Maglie.

Larsen sent the first three Dodgers down in order. Jackie Robinson, opening the second inning, smashed a vicious grounder off Andy Carey's glove at third base, but McDougald recovered it in time for the put-out.

Inning after inning, Handsome Don kept the Brooks from reaching first. The Yankees picked up a run off Maglie in the fourth on Mantle's homer and Gil Hodges almost followed suit for the Dodgers in the fifth, but Mantle, streaking into deep left center, tore across the turf to nail the ball at the fence.

Sandy Amoros, the next batter, threw a scare into the thousands at the Stadium and the millions watching on TV when he tagged a towering drive toward the right field stands which curved foul at the very last moment.

Berra let out the deepest sigh. He was surprised at himself for feeling so shaky when Larsen, the man who was pitching the perfect game so far, seemed so calm and detached. True to baseball tradition, no one said a word about the no-hitter in the Yankee dugout.

Bauer singled Carey home in the sixth for the second Yankee run and Larsen, working like a well-oiled machine, kept grinding the Dodgers down. In the eighth, Hodges caught one on the end of his bat, a screamer toward third, but Carey nabbed it with a lunging catch.

Not a Dodger had reached first base, by hit, walk or error. Now it was the ninth inning, the crowd strangely silent and the tension so heavy on the field that it almost hurt physically. The tight, lined faces of the Yankees revealed their feelings.

Only Larsen, by this time fully aware of the enormity of the feat, maintained his composure. Berra understood what

torment must have been contained inside the huge pitcher:
the need to preserve control over singing nerves, to push
back all thoughts but those needed to get the next few men
out.

Larsen got Furillo and then Campy for the first two outs.
He was one out away from baseball immortality—the first
perfect no-hit game ever pitched in World Series history.

Burt Shotton, the Dodger manager, had to make the
effort, even if he himself might have been rooting for Larsen at this point. He sent Dale Mitchell in to pinch-hit for
Maglie.

Complete silence descended on the Stadium as Larsen
worked on the big former Cleveland slugger. Both benches
had stopped their chattering. The tension was brutal.

Without preliminary windup, as he had done all through
this incredible game, Larsen pitched. Strike one, as the ball
nipped the corner. The crowd gasped in relief.

The next pitch was a ball, Mitchell watching a curve
miss the plate. Yogi was worried. He knew Mitchell as a
hard, level swinger from his days with the Indians.

"Keep it low and inside," Yogi told himself over and
over. Mitchell could murder the outside pitch.

Berra gave his signal and Larsen's arm went into action
again.

Mitchell swung and missed, a curve breaking inside over
the knees for strike two.

How much more could Don take? Yogi wondered, noting
Larsen's haggard look. It had to be this one, the kid's tiring
fast.

It was up to Berra now. Should he call for a waste pitch,
gambling that Mitchell would be swinging away? Or should
it be the low, inside curve? He studied Mitchell, resolutely
swinging his bat, strong and fresh, his eyes clear. Then he
knew what it had to be.

Yogi signaled. Larsen nodded and put his foot on the rubber.

The pitch came in, low and close. Mitchell swung.

He missed!

Strike three and it was over, a perfect game for Larsen and a 2–0 victory for the Yankees to put them ahead of Brooklyn, three games to two, in the series.

In the clubhouse, after escaping the pandemonium on the field, Berra sagged against his locker. He was spent; his hands trembled and he gulped air in nervous relief.

It was late but Yogi had neither the desire nor the strength to leave. The ordeal with the reporters was almost as exhausting as the game itself.

Bauer, fully dressed, sauntered by. "That was smart, being Larsen's catcher," Hank said. "Now you'll go down in the record books." He shook his head in mock admiration. "Yes sir, real smart. . . ."

No one had to kid Berra about his role in the perfect game. Everyone knew what his catching, his knowledge of the batters, his ability to inspire confidence and relax the pitcher meant.

Yogi was also on the firing line the next day at Ebbets Field as Bob Turley went to work on the Dodgers in what for a while seemed to be a repeat performance. With the same no-windup style, Turley struck out eleven and allowed only three hits going into the tenth inning in a bitter duel with Clem Labine.

Twice Berra got on, once with a double and again with a single, but twice Labine stranded him there. In the Dodger half of the tenth, Clem popped out but Junior Gilliam walked. Reese sacrificed the runner to second and Turley was ordered to walk Snider.

Robinson was up, one of the most dangerous clutch hitters in baseball. Jackie fouled off the first pitch, let the next one go for a ball and leaned into the third for a drive to left field. Slaughter ran in a few steps, then futilely tried to backpedal as the ball shot over his head. Gilliam raced home with the run for the 1–0 triumph.

The Yankees stormed into their quarters in a raging mood. Turley had pitched his heart out for them and they hadn't produced a run for him.

Yogi slammed his mask into his locker in disgust. It was a rough one to lose for Bob, he thought. The squat catcher walked over to the downcast Turley.

"Sorry, Bob," Yogi said. "You pitched great. We were just bums behind you today."

Turley looked up with a tired smile. "No," he said shaking his head. "I got up four times, too, and drew a blank. Labine was great. He beat us. He beat me."

So once again it was down to the seventh and final game in a World Series with the Brooklyn Dodgers. This was the team, Yogi thought bitterly, that beat the Yankees in the seventh game last year. It had to be different this time.

"Carmen," Yogi said as he kissed his wife good-by the morning of October 10th, "I feel lucky today—home run lucky."

Carmen pursed her lips prettily. "Is that because Newcombe is pitching today?" she asked, a smile dancing in her eyes.

It stopped Yogi. It still amazed him when she showed a flash of subtle baseball knowledge. "Maybe that's it," he said thoughtfully. "I never figured it that way." He kissed her again and drove off toward Brooklyn and the fateful game in Ebbets Field.

Newcombe was on the mound and throwing bullets again. For the Yankees, it was young, lean Johnny Kucks.

The fireworks started immediately. Bauer opened with a single, but Newk fanned Martin and Mantle. Yogi fouled off two pitches, then larruped the next over the right field barrier into Bedford Avenue for a two-run homer.

In the third inning, Martin singled, but Mantle whiffed for the second time.

Yogi was at the plate again, smiling at the gangling pitcher. Newk worked him carefully for two strikes and one ball when it happened. Berra caught one on the nose and the ball went hurtling into Bedford Avenue again for two more runs.

Elston Howard's homer chased Newk in the fourth and Bill Skowron's grand slammer in the seventh sent Craig to the showers.

When it was over the Yankees had won, 9–0, and the series was over, the world championship back in the Bronx for the seventeenth time.

"It was wonderful," Yogi exulted later. Three homers for him in the series and a .360 batting average.

He had set a new series record for runs batted in, with ten, and caught more series games (forty-five) than any other catcher in the game.

How long could this go on? Here was a question all baseball was asking, not only of Berra but of the Yankees.

"Every year," Yogi insisted. "After all, I'm only thirty-one."

But even he knew somewhere in the back of his mind that Father Time was taking longer strides after him now.

Yogi shrugged it off. "I feel great," he insisted. "Better than ever. For Pete's sake, is thirty-one old?"

The next season might tell.

· 19 ·

The huge crowd in Cleveland's Municipal Stadium let out a concerted gasp, then fell strangely silent as Yogi Berra sank slowly to his knees over home plate, blood gushing in torrents from his face.

Even the players stood momentarily stunned after the crunching impact of the foul tip which had sliced back and right through the catcher's mask.

For a long second everyone watched Yogi clutch agonizingly at his face, the blood streaming through his fingers.

Then, the hush broken, a crowd surged around Yogi.

It was the third inning of a game with the Indians the night of June 5, 1957. Bobby Shantz, the tiny left-hander, was pitching for the Yankees when Larry Raines barely flicked a waist-high fast ball, caroming it off with increased force directly into Berra's mask.

The iron bar across the face guard snapped at both ends and slammed across Yogi's nose like a hammer blow. It was a freak accident, a one-in-a-million shot, but there was the Yankee backstop doubled up on his knees with Trainer Gus Mauch vainly trying to stanch the flow of blood.

Yogi, dazed, felt the searing pain across his nose and through his eyes and dimly he became aware of the sticky wetness on his chin and fingers and chest.

It was not until after he was helped into the dressing room and placed on the rubbing table that he could begin to discern the worried faces hovering over him.

"I'm all right, I'm all right," he mumbled through thick, swollen lips. Dr. Harry Haller, a Cleveland physician and friend of Mauch's, worked to halt the hemorrhage.

"Did I go down?" Yogi asked vaguely. Someone said he hadn't and he attempted a grin. His nose, obviously broken, was puffed to twice its normal size and both eyes were beginning to show discoloration and swelling.

"Hey, I gotta call Carmen," Yogi remembered suddenly, lifting up on his elbow. "She must've seen the game on TV and she'll be worried stiff. You know how it looks on TV. . . ."

He made the call from the hospital. X rays and further examination revealed a clean break of the nose with no damage to the eyes or surrounding areas.

"It's too bad," Yogi mused the next morning. "I might've got some hits last night."

He had read how his Yankee mates, going berserk with their bats after the accident, had clubbed the Tribe into submission, 13–3. It had been a sour spring for both Berra and the Bombers.

Everything seemed to have gone wrong. The Copacabana incident . . . his own inexplicable batting slump . . . the Yankees floundering behind the White Sox and Indians in the pennant race . . . just a mess.

The funny thing, Yogi thought, was that he had been clobbering the ball in preseason training down south and never felt better. Or hit better, he reflected bitterly. He had batted .340 before the 1957 season opened.

The American League campaign started wonderfully, with Berra walloping two hits, one a homer, against the Senators. After that, the road was sharply downhill. By May

3rd, Yogi was batting a puny .200 and the Yanks were a game and a half behind Chicago.

He remembered his thirty-second birthday—Sunday, May 12th—and the boys kidding him about getting old. They beat Baltimore, 4–3, at the Stadium and Yogi was whitewashed, ending a streak of eleven consecutive games in which he had hit safely.

The streak meant nothing, Yogi knew. He was batting .216, a disgraceful figure. Things didn't improve, either for him or any of the Yankees.

May 16th was Billy Martin's twenty-ninth birthday. "It's my party," he said, inviting Berra, Bauer, Ford, Mantle, Kucks and their wives to the Copacabana night club.

There had been a senseless incident . . . an insult . . . bouncers hustling someone out . . . then the newspapers splashing it all over the land that Bauer was being charged with punching a delicatessen owner who popped off to the husky former Marine.

The Yankee brass was incensed and even Casey Stengel, who knew how badly his slumping, worried ballplayers needed the break from routine, was caught in the middle. Fines of one thousand dollars each were plastered on the players, only Kucks getting off with five hundred dollars. A month later, Martin was traded to Kansas City.

It wouldn't have been so bad, Yogi thought, if the boys had been able to hit after that. He shuddered at the headlines: Berra Called Yankee Key . . . Team To Jell When Yogi Starts Hitting . . . Berra's Slump Hurting Mantle's Batting Average.

A foul tip off Don Zimmer's bat bruised Berra's ankle in a Mayor's Trophy charity game against the Dodgers on May 23rd to add to the catcher's general woes. The Bombers struggled along the same dismal way, with or without him.

Going into a night game on June 5th in Cleveland, the Yankees trailed the White Sox by five games in the pennant race. After Yogi's accident, the gap widened to six games by June 8th and Casey became desperate. He changed his batting order every day, shifted players and tried every trick of psychology he knew.

The upswing came gradually for the Yankees, who finally made it to the top for good on the last day of June after a series sweep against Kansas City.

But Yankee success was not Berra success. He still wasn't hitting. While doctors insisted the broken nose did not impair his vison, Yogi knew he wasn't seeing well at the plate. He wasn't sleeping well, either.

"I can't breathe through this thing," he said, fingering his flattened proboscis. "I keep waking up nights. I'm tired."

In July, just before the All-Star game in St. Louis, Yogi was hitting a meager .230. He occasionally returned to brief flashes of his old batting form, as on July 3rd when he drove in eight runs against Boston with a homer, two singles and a long fly nabbed against the fence by Jackie Jensen.

He caught Jim Bunning, sensational Detroit rookie hurler, in the All-Star contest, won, 6–5, by the American League, and batted in a run, his first ever in his nine mid-season classic appearances. But otherwise he was a bust.

Finally, yielding to Carmen's pleas, Yogi visited an oculist and discovered a tendency to farsightedness. "It could be the reason you don't see the ball clearly when it approaches the plate," he was told.

Yogi ordered eyeglasses. "I'll wear 'em for the movies or TV," he conceded. "You know, rest my eyes and see what happens."

As his batting did not improve, Berra decided to try the spectacles during batting practice. It was sheer desperation.

Stengel was willing to go along with his slumping catcher because the Yankees were winging now and comfortably ahead.

The glasses arrived July 13th, steel-rimmed panes that looked monstrous to the sensitive Berra.

Yogi wore them out to batting practice, feeling self-conscious and awkward. He knew the merciless riding he was in for once the glasses were spotted. His worst fears were realized when he emerged from the dugout to take batting practice in Kansas City.

"They haven't helped your looks any," someone hooted, "and you could use help."

Yogi curled up inside but put on a brave grin. "Aw, I think they make me look kind of dignified," he said.

"Hey, Ump," Irv Noren shouted, "don't you see so good?" The players sometimes called Berra "Ump" because of his penchant to make his own calls on balls and strikes along with the men in blue.

"I see better than you," Yogi retorted.

All through the session, players from both teams ragged him until he felt he would swing a bat at the next taunter. He expected to take a kidding, but had underestimated his own sensitivity.

"I don't care," he told Whitey Ford later, "if only they help me get some hits."

At first Yogi didn't wear the specs during games, but as his slump continued the stocky little backstop decided to give it a try. His whole game was falling apart. He was weary, anxious and irritable.

"The guy is tired, I know," Stengel told Dan Daniel of the New York *World-Telegram and Sun*. "He needs a few days' rest, but with Harry Simpson still needed at first base and Tony Kubek at short, I can't take Elston Howard from the outfield to spell Yogi behind the bat."

By the middle of August no one spoke about Berra's slump any longer. He still was down at .230 and the thought ran through the dugouts and press boxes that perhaps Yogi wasn't merely in a slump, that he was just a .230 hitter now.

Whether it could be blamed on the foul tip which smashed his nose and possibly affected his vision, or the heavy toll of day-in, day-out catching, no longer was the point.

"Why do you keep him in?" Stengel was asked.

The questioner got a withering look from the manager. "Because he's the best doggoned catcher in the game," Casey spat out. "You see the way he handles those pitchers? Besides, Yogi'll come out of it."

Stengel's prophecy was borne out a week later. Shedding his glasses, Yogi began to hit. In six days his batting average climbed to .245 and his good-natured grin was restored. Life was worth living again.

"It wasn't my eyes," he analyzed. "I just wasn't whipping the bat around. Maybe I was tired and didn't know it. You know, this season isn't over yet."

His batting climb was halted on September 6th in Washington when a foul tip bashed in his right thumb. It bothered him almost to the last game of the campaign and he finished up with a .251 mark, lowest of his major league career.

He had found the home run range late in September, however, to wind up with twenty-four round-trippers and eighty-two runs batted in.

Yogi's lifetime record after eleven full seasons in the major leagues still was remarkable. His batting average was .290, with 1085 runs driven in and 262 homers, a record for catchers.

Yogi went into the 1957 World Series against the Milwaukee Braves as chipper and hopeful as he ever had been, buoyed by his gratifying September surge.

But, alas, while he turned in a top-notch performance, the Yankees were not destined to win. Milwaukee fans, hysterical at winning the series for the first time, went wild when the Braves copped the championship in seven games.

Yogi collected eight hits for a .320 series mark, hammered a homer, drew four walks and drove in two runs, but like most of his teammates he could do nothing with Lew Burdette. The Milwaukee hurler defeated the mighty Bombers three times—the last two by shutouts—and that was the difference.

For the first time since Berra had come up, a dumpy, clownish catcher with a phenomenal batting eye, the Yankees had reason to worry about the position for next season.

Yogi knew it but refused to bridle at rumors of a pay cut. When the Yankees offered him a slightly reduced contract of fifty-eight thousand dollars for 1958, Yogi quickly signed.

"I had a bad year," he conceded after the signing. "Every player has a bad season once in a while."

"Suppose you had another bad one in 1958?" a reporter asked.

"I guess I'd quit if that happened," Yogi answered slowly. "Or maybe they'd trade me."

Carmen, standing nearby, shuddered at the thought. "Let's not even think about another bad year," she said. "I'm sure it will be a good one."

Eyeglasses were out, Yogi revealed. "I don't need 'em," he said.

"He never did in the first place," Carmen added.

Bigger things in the financial world were happening for Berra at this time. The immense bowling establishment which he and his partner Phil Rizzuto, now retired as a player but broadcasting Yankee games, had built in Clifton, New Jersey, was ready for business.

There were two openings of the million-dollar enterprise with its forty bowling alleys, its cocktail bar, its restaurant and nursery. The nursery, Yogi explained, was for folks who wanted to park the kiddies somewhere while they bowled.

He knew about kiddies. His third son, Dale, had joined the family in December of 1956.

The establishment opened for business in February, but the second and "grand" opening was reserved for April when the Yankees, at home in New York, could attend in force and give the business a gala send-off.

St. Petersburg seemed the same to Yogi in the spring of 1958. The sun was warm and strong, the skies bright and blue, the air balmy. "I feel great," he announced.

Stengel had the needle out early. He knew Berra and what it took to stimulate him. "Yogi may be a .250 hitter the rest of his life," Casey intoned. "There is no certainty he can make a comeback."

To which a smiling Yogi said, "Oh, yeah?"

At thirty-three, Berra was by no means finished. For all the arduous work he had put in, playing in 1,474 games for a catcher's record over twelve years, Yogi was still a sturdy, healthy man endowed with great muscular strength and good reflexes.

Bill Dickey, his old mentor who had left the club after a siege of nervous exhaustion in 1957, retained his faith in the man who had come such a long way from The Hill.

"He has plenty of good years left in him," Dickey said from his home in Little Rock, Arkansas. "Yogi is the best catcher in baseball today and he'll stay on top for quite a while yet."

Yogi was inclined to agree with the man who had molded him into an outstanding receiver.

"You can't argue with a guy like Bill," he said, smiling. "After all, who knows as much about catching as Dickey?"

No one answered until a gentle, throaty voice said, "You do."

It was Carmen, proudly taking her stand for her man. Yogi laughed and put his arm around his attractive wife. "You've never been wrong, dear," he said.

LAWRENCE PETER (YOGI) BERRA

Born, May 12, 1925   Height—5' 8"   Weight—192

Year	Club	League	G	AB	R	H	2B	3B	HR	RBI	BA	BB	SO
1943	Norfolk Pied. L.		111	376	52	95	17	8	7	56	.253	30	30
1944-45	Kansas City A. A.						(In U. S. Navy)						
1946	Newark I. L.		77	277	41	87	14	1	15	59	.314	16	16
1946	New York A. L.		7	22	3	8	1	0	2	4	.364	1	1
1947	New York A. L.		83	293	41	82	15	3	11	54	.280	13	12
1948	New York A. L.		125	469	70	143	24	10	14	98	.305	25	24
1949	New York A. L.		116	415	59	115	20	2	20	91	.277	22	25
1950	New York A. L.		151	597	116	192	30	6	28	124	.322	55	12
1951	New York A. L.		141	547	92	161	19	4	27	88	.294	44	20
1952	New York A. L.		142	534	97	146	17	1	30	98	.273	66	24
1953	New York A. L.		137	503	80	149	23	5	27	108	.296	50	32
1954	New York A. L.		151	584	88	179	28	6	22	125	.307	56	29
1955	New York A. L.		147	541	84	147	20	3	27	108	.272	60	20
1956	New York A. L.		140	521	93	155	29	2	30	105	.298	65	29
1957	New York A. L.		134	482	74	121	14	2	24	82	.251	57	24
	Major League Totals		1474	5508	897	1598	240	44	262	1085	.290	514	252

WORLD SERIES RECORD

Year	Club	League	G	AB	R	H	2B	3B	HR	RBI	BA	BB	SO
1947	New York	A. L.	6	19	2	3	0	0	1	2	.158	1	2
1949	New York	A. L.	4	16	2	1	0	0	0	1	.063	1	3
1950	New York	A. L.	4	15	2	3	0	0	1	2	.200	2	1
1951	New York	A. L.	6	23	4	6	1	0	0	0	.261	2	1
1952	New York	A. L.	7	28	2	6	1	0	2	3	.214	2	4
1953	New York	A. L.	6	21	3	9	1	0	1	4	.429	3	3
1955	New York	A. L.	7	24	5	10	1	0	1	2	.417	3	1
1956	New York	A. L.	7	25	5	9	2	0	3	10	.360	4	1
1957	New York	A. L.	7	25	5	8	1	0	1	2	.320	4	0
World Series Totals			54	196	30	55	7	0	10	26	.281	22	16

ALL-STAR GAME RECORD

Year	League	AB	R	H	2B	3B	HR	RBI	BA	BB	SO
1949	American	3	0	0	0	0	0	0	.000	0	0
1950	American	2	0	0	0	0	0	0	.000	0	0
1951	American	4	1	1	0	0	0	0	.250	0	0
1952	American	2	0	0	0	0	0	0	.000	0	0
1953	American	4	0	0	0	0	0	0	.000	0	0
1954	American	4	2	2	0	0	0	0	.500	1	0
1955	American	6	1	1	0	0	0	0	.167	0	0
1956	American	2	0	2	0	0	0	0	1.000	0	0
1957	American	3	0	1	0	0	0	1	.333	1	0
All-Star Game Totals		30	4	7	0	0	0	1	.233	2	0

Note: Berra was selected on the 1948 All-Star team, but did not play.

Index